THE PLOW
DISARMARMENT
1980-&

Edited by Arthur J. Laffin

Foreword by Daniel Berrigan, S.J.

First printing

ISBN # 0-9636224-8-X
Plowshares Chronicle

Book design by Erin Leitner-Sieber

ROSE HILL BOOKS

In loving memory of Philip Berrigan

ACKNOWLEDGMENTS

This book is about a special group of peacemakers who have tried to incarnate the biblical prophecy to beat the swords (weapons) of our time into plowshares. I express deep gratitude to each person whose acts of nonviolent resistance made this book possible.

I am deeply thankful to all those who helped make this book a reality. I am very grateful to Paul Magno for his steadfast support of this book and his tireless efforts to arrange for its publication.

I am also very grateful to Erin Leitner-Sieber for doing the entire layout of the book. I am deeply thankful for his heartfelt support and for the outstanding work he did to make this book possible.

I am also very grateful to Susan Crane for her special contribution of proofreading this book.

I am especially thankful to all those who supported the publication of this book, including Dan Berrigan, Pat McSweeney, Anne Montgomery, Elmer Maas, Dorothy Day Catholic Worker, and Jonah House.

Finally, I want to pay tribute to all victims of violence and war, the disappeared, the tortured, the forgotten prisoners of conscience and the martyrs. I honor, too, all peacemakers throughout history-past and present-who have conspired to keep alive the way of non-violence and uphold Gods command "Thou shalt not kill", without counting the cost. Deo Gratias for their gift of courage and fidelity to the truth.

Arthur Laffin

CONTENTS

FOREWORD

Q: WHAT'S IN A NAME?
A: EVERYTHING IT SEEMS!

We were locked in a dilemma, eight of us, as summer tipped into fall of 1980. We had met for months of prayer and discussion. But try as we might, one matter still escaped us. What to name our newborn resolve (or better, our not-quite born resolve)?

Naming things, creation, children--naming aright, without equivocation or lying or double dealing - this was a Hebrew task, a biblical task to be sure. The thought was vaguely consoling.

According to our Bible, the 'name' must go beyond itself, mean something, connect. It must evoke a tradition, a vocation, a task in the world--a gift (even a wildly difficult one!). It must hint at community desire, passion, hands-on conscience. It must (and here one's knees turned to water at the effrontery of the claim) - it must bespeak prophecy.

Prophecy. Meaning what? Something quite simple; truth telling, reading aright what Jesus called 'the signs of the times'.

What most Americans took horridly for granted as 'normal'-- nuclear weapons studding the earth like the sores of Job, the Pentagon squatting monstrously on the land, brooding, hatching its hellish eggs, its invasions, bombings (add in year 2002 a plague of depleted uranium, sanctions throttling the Iraqi children). Quite simply, these could not be taken as 'normal' acts of a civilized people.

Our Bible, our Christ said a stern nay. Such behavior was in sum (and remains) the multiplied follies of ethical dwarfs.

We knew it in our bones. That as yet unnamed 'name' of our action must echo the primordial nay.

On that late summer day, 1980, a momentous breakthrough occurred. It came as I recall, through Molly Rush, grandmother, founder of the Thomas Merton Center in Pittsburgh. At her suggestion, we opened our Bibles and took a close look at Isaiah 2: 'They shall beat their swords into plowshares'.

That day the name was named. The 'child,' our purpose, was born--born with a name, as was only right and fitting.

Since autumn of 1980, the child, the purpose, 'Swords into Plowshares' has flourished, in a modest fashion, throughout the U.S., in Europe and Australia. This book, its photos and text carefully assembled by Arthur Laffin, tells the story.

And quite a story it is. Many brothers and sisters have followed on the birth of the first. Each and all bears a strong family resemblance, outlook, bearing - passion even. Each is skilled in decoding the weathers, taking soundings of land, sea, air, space itself --that skill commended (one dares venture, conferred) by Christ. Each reading aright the signs of the times. Each declaring in an audacious drama of spirit and integrity and verse and risk; Not In My Name!

And each of course, paying up. In hard time and easy, in time undergone and time served. All said, in the theory and painful praxis of--the human.

This little book, be it noted, is open ended. For 22 years, judges and prosecutors and sheriffs and wardens, rattling their cuffs and pounding their gavels, have declared that the audacity, the impudence, the nimiety--the Plowshares 'crimes' in sum--that these stop, here and now. Halt, here and now. Make sure, pour on juridical scorn and spleen, punishment, suppression of evidence, of conscience, of international law. Conduct and (entirely legal) Bible burning.

These punishing eminences are of course, woefully wide the mark.

Reality smiles up its sleeve. Our little book is open ended.

Daniel Berrigan, S.J.

AN INTRODUCTION TO PLOWSHARES DISARMAMENT ACTIONS

by Arthur Laffin

In this article, I would like to give a brief background of plowshares actions, reflect on the underlying spirit and hope of these actions, address how the courts have responded, and briefly address some of the major criticisms about these actions. It is my intent here not to be exhaustive on covering all these issues in great detail, but to give the reader a general sense of what plowshares-disarmament actions are about.

On September 9, 1980, the "Plowshares Eight" carried out the first of what have come to be known as plowshares actions. Eight peacemakers entered the General Electric plant in King of Prussia, Pennsylvania, where the nose cones from the Mark 12-A nuclear warheads were manufactured. With hammers and blood they enacted the biblical prophecies of Isaiah (2:4) and Micah (4:3) to "*beat swords into plowshares*" by hammering on two of the nose cones and pouring blood on documents. Thus, the name "plowshares" has been used to identify this action. The eight were subsequently arrested and tried by a jury, convicted and sentenced to prison terms ranging from 1 ½ to 10 years. After a series of appeals that lasted 10 years, they were resentenced to time served—from several days to 17 ½ months.

Since the Plowshares Eight action, others, acting individually and in community, have entered military bases and weapons facilities and have symbolically and actually disarmed components of U.S. first-strike nuclear weapons systems: the MX, Perishing II, Cruise, Minuteman ICBM's, Trident II missiles, Trident submarines, B-52 bombers, P-3 Orion anti-submarine aircraft, the Navstar system, the ELF communication system, the Milstar satellite system, a nuclear capable battleship and the Aegis destroyer. Combat aircraft used for military intervention such as the F-111 fighter bomber, the F-15A fighter, the F-18 bomber, the A-10 Warthog, the Hawk aircraft, as well as combat helicopters and other conventional weapons, including aircraft missile launchers, bazookas, grenade throwers, and AK-5 automatic rifles, have been disarmed. Model weapons have been disarmed at an "Arms Bazaar." People who have been involved in plowshares actions have undertaken a process of intense spiritual preparation, nonviolence training and community formation, and have given careful consideration to the risks involved. Plowshares activists, accepting full responsibility for their actions, remain at the site of their action so that they can publicly explain their witness.

Resonating closely with this spirit of nonviolent direct disarmament, other people, though not seeing their action arising out of the biblical prophecy of Isaiah and Micah, have been compelled to nonviolently disarm components of nuclear and conventional weapons. Although individuals who have carried out these actions have been inspired by plowshares participants who embrace a biblical vision, they view their action as being primarily motivated by a deeply held conscience commitment to nonviolence or by other spiritual or moral convictions.

As of February 2003, more than 150 individuals have participated in over 75 plowshares and related disarmament actions. Also several groups and individuals were stopped by security and arrested at or near a weapons site before being able to complete their intended disarmament action. Some plowshares activists have gone on to participate in other plowshares actions. Plowshares actions have occurred in the U.S., Australia, German, Holland, Sweden, Ireland, and England. The backgrounds of plowshares activists vary widely. Parents, grandparents, veterans, lawyers, teachers, artists, musicians, priests, sisters, house-painters, carpenters, writers, health-care workers, students, advocates for the poor and homeless, and members of Catholic Worker communities have all participated in plowshares actions. Most of those who have participated in plowshares actions remain actively involved in the peace and justice movement.

In my view, the basic hope of the plowshares actions (and here I'm not attempting to speak for other people involved in these actions) is to communicate from the moment of entry into a plant or base—and throughout the court process and prison witness—and underlying faith that the power of nonviolent love can overcome the forces of violence; a reverence for the sacredness of all life and creation; a plea for justice for victims of poverty, the arms race and economic sanctions; an acceptance of personal responsibility for the dismantling and the physical conversion of the weapons; and a spiritual conversion of the heart to the way of justice and reconciliation. Thus, plowshares participants believe that the physical dismantling of the weapon and the personal disarmament of the heart is a reciprocal process. As Philip Berrigan states: *"We try to disarm ourselves by disarming the weapons."*

The main symbols used in plowshares actions are hammers and blood. Hammers are used to literally begin the process of disarmament that thousands of talks and numerous treaties have failed to accomplish. The hammer is used to take apart as well as create, and to point to the urgency for conversion of war production to products that enhance life. The blood symbolizes the mass killing that weapons of mass destruction can inflict, as well as the murderous cost they now impose on the poor. Blood speaks too of human unity and the willingness to give one's life rather than to take life.

Seeking to expose the violence, secrecy, and idolatry of the national security state, some plowshares defendants have tried to present a "justification" or "necessity" defense. During their defense they have tried to show, through personal and expert witness testimony, that their actions were morally and legally justified and that their intent was to protect life. In most cases, the courts have shown their complicity in protecting the interests of the government and have disallowed this defense. Some plowshares groups have also presented a defense declaring that a state religion of "nuclearism" has been established, which is unconstitutional, in violation of the First Amendment. Moreover, nuclearism is in violation of God's law, which forbids the worship of "gods of metal." Plowshares defendants have moved for dismissal of all charges brought against them; for the law, as applied in these cases, is used to protect this unconstitutional state religion. Such motions have been consistently denied.

THE PLOWSHARES CHRONOLOGY 1980-2003
[3]

With the exception of the G.E. 5, the Aegis Plowshares, the first Australian Plowshares action, and the Earth and Space Plowshares action, all plowshares activists have been prosecuted for their actions. While most plowshares-disarmament activists have pled not guilty and have gone to trial, several opted to plead "no contest" or "guilty" to charges brought against them. Most of the trials to date, mainly jury trials, have ended in convictions. However, members of the Epiphany Plowshares were tried an unprecedented five times with three trials ending in hung juries and mistrials. Also, Chris Cole's first trial for a plowshares action in England ended in a hung jury. Also the first ever acquittal in a plowshares case occurred in Liverpool, England where a jury found the Seeds of Hope—East Timor Ploughshares not guilty. There was also another plowshares acquittal, which occurred in Edinburgh, Scotland during the trial of three women who disarmed Trident-related technology as part of the Trident Ploughshares 2000 campaign. And in another plowshares-disarmament action against Trident in England, a trial for two women ended in a hung jury for one charge and an acquittal for the second charge.

During the trials in the U.S., which have occurred in both state and federal courts, most of the defendants have represented themselves and have been assisted by legal advisers. The trial tactics by judges and government prosecutors have become extremely repressive. A "Motion In Limine," which calls for the complete prohibition of "affirmative" defenses, has been introduced in a number of plowshares trials. For example, prior to the third and fourth trials of the Epiphany Plowshares, the trial judge, complying with the U.S. prosecutor's request, imposed a "gag" order forbidding any mention of such subjects as God's law, the Bible, international law, U.S. military intervention in Central America, nuclear weapons and the poor. For speaking about these subjects, two defendants were given contempt charges and 20-day jail sentences. And during their opening statement to the jury in North Carolina, members of the Pax Christi-Spirit of Life Plowshares were found in contempt of court for not complying with the judge's instruction to refrain from speaking about crimes of the national security state and their moral and legal intent.

Prison sentences have varied for each plowshares-disarmament action. These sentences have ranged from suspended sentences to 18 years. The average sentence for plowshares activists has been between one and two years.

Doing support work on behalf of plowshares activists has also been an integral part of the plowshares actions. Efforts by local support groups have been invaluable in supporting plowshares activists during trial and imprisonment and in helping to educate the public about the meaning of these actions. As people have been sentenced to long prison terms, support for prisoners and their families has been, and continues to be, crucial.

Throughout the 23-year history of the plowshares actions, questions have been raised regarding different aspects of these actions. Some have voiced concerns that these actions are violent because property, in this case a weapon, has been damaged. Plowshares activists believe that nuclear weapons and all weapons of war are anti-God, anti-life, and therefore, are inherently evil and have no right to exist. Thus, it is the responsibility of people of faith and conscience to begin to nonviolently dismantle these weapons. In the Trident Nein plowshares action, which I participated, we hammered and poured blood on missile hatches and sonar equipment of the first-strike Trident submarine. With spray-paint we renamed the Trident "USS Auschwitz," because of our belief that such a weapon has no more right to exist than the Nazi gas ovens. Would trying to take apart a gas oven be considered an act of violence or vandalism? I believe that it would not. Would it be consistent with nonviolence? I believe so. Plowshares participants believe that trying to dismantle a weapon of mass murder is not an act of violence even though the media and the courts characterize these acts as "vandalism" and various other crimes, rather than as an act of disarmament. The real crime is not the hammering upon weapons, but the U.S. government's first-strike nuclear policy, its military interventionist policy, and its commitment to wage a war against the poor of the world to protect its economic interests.

People have also questioned whether these actions are truly nonviolent because of the secrecy that surrounds the action. Plowshares people contend that no advance notice is needed to disarm an illegal weapon that has no right to exist in the first place. (Did Jesus give advance notice to authorities when he cleansed the temple? Did abolitionists give advance notice to government officials about harboring slaves?) People have a moral and legal right to begin the disarmament process at any base or factory at any time. They posses this right because they honor and try to embody God's law, which authorities and personnel break consistently by their work. There is therefore, no moral or political duty to inform or dialogue with them about a witness beforehand. The witness is the dialogue.

Moreover, once the action occurs there is no attempt to conceal the truth of what happened. Plowshares people take full responsibility for their action by awaiting arrest, telling the story of their action in court and to the public, as well as speaking out from jail and prison.

Also, in the past the government has charged peace activists and plowshares participants with conspiracy charges. Great care is taken prior to each action to avoid exposing others to the risk of such charges. It seems to me that this approach, while different from other nonviolent actions, reflects the spirit of biblical nonviolence.

There have also been important concerns raised about the need for what disarmament activist Peter Lumsdaine calls a more "effective strategic resistance" approach to the weapons rather than the mostly symbolic approach of plowshares actions. (1) This approach, which centers on committing "maximum" damage to key weapons systems (i.e. Navstar) in order to render them ineffective, has certainly provoked a meaningful dialogue—one which continues. While plowshares activists have different perspectives on this issue, most would undoubtedly agree with the following viewpoint articulated by Philip Berrigan:

Plowshares began disarmament in 1980, doing what the government refused to do for 35 years. With equal concern, Plowshares appealed to the hearts, minds and spirits of the American people—'You must share disarmament!' The twin goals of Plowshares—symbolic yet real disarmament and sharing disarmament—have reciprocity. The weapons exist because our fear, violence and hatred built them. Plowshares must address these realities...

The hammer is a modest tool and a potent symbol, which within the context of Isaiah's prophecy, insists upon a universal responsibility for justice and peace. But it also confines us within human limits—we are not superpeople, nor do we embody the fantasies of Hollywood or the Washington plutocrats. The imperative is to be human in an inhuman time, to act in season and out despite the prospect that the American empire might not break up in our lifetime, nor disarmament happen while we live. If that be the case, modesty of means will sustain us as another face of faith. And faith is not faith except for the long haul. (2)

Regarding this notion of faith, Elizabeth McAlister asserts:

There is not going to be any real disarmament until there's a disarming of hearts. And so one puts oneself on the line to symbolically, but really, disarm the weapons in a hope and prayer that the action might be used by the Spirit of God to change minds and hearts. One puts oneself on the line—at risk and in jeopardy—to communicate the depth of commitment to that hope. (3)

Based on my experience, it is important to note that each of the plowshares participants I've met has carefully reflected on these and other important considerations prior to an action. While there does exist among plowshares participants a basic unanimity about the underlying spirit for plowshares actions, there is a diversity of opinion among plowshares participants about certain issues including defenses to use in court, the level of cooperation with court and probation authorities, and the payment of fines and restitution. Clearly, these and other issues that I have addressed have generated important discussion among plowshares activists and the wider disarmament movement.

In the final analysis, people who do plowshares actions are ordinary people who, with all their weaknesses, are attempting to respond in faith and conscience to a moral mandate, which must be enacted in our violent world. These actions are not to be glamorized or taken lightly. People have taken great risks, experienced the loneliness and dehumanization of prison, and have had to cope with many difficult personal and family hardships. Building and sustaining an acting community takes extraordinary commitment and is certainly not problem-free. Yet, with all their limitations and imperfections, these actions are a powerful reminder that we can live in a world without weapons and war if people are willing to begin the process of disarmament by literally beating the swords (weapons) of our time in plowshares. While these actions are deemed criminal by the state, they should be considered, in light of the great evil we face, the norm. Although each plowshares action has many similarities to others, in the end each is unique, each is a learning process, each is an experiment in truth.

NOTES

1. For a further explanation of the "effective strategic resistance" approach see article by Peter Lumsdaine in The Nuclear Resister, October 7, 1992
2. Berrigan, Philip, The Nuclear Resister, December 23, 1992
3. McAlister, Elizabeth, The Catholic Agitator, November, 1992

*"And they shall beat their swords into plowshares,
and their spears into pruning hooks;
nation shall not lift up sword against nation,
neither shall they learn war anymore."*

Isaiah 2:4

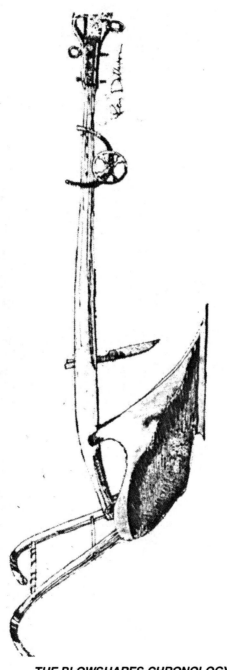

THE PLOWSHARES CHRONOLOGY 1980-2003
[10]

THE PLOWSHARES DISARMARMENT CHRONOLOGY
1980-2003

THE PLOWSHARES CHRONOLOGY 1980-2003
[11]

PLOWSHARES EIGHT: September 9, 1980 Daniel Berrigan, Jesuit priest, author and poet from New York City; Philip Berrigan, father and co-founder of Jonah House in Baltimore, MD; Dean Hammer, member of the Covenant Peace Community in New Haven, CT; Elmer Maas, musician and former college teacher from New York City; Carl Kabat, Oblate priest and missionary; Anne Montgomery, Religious of the Sacred Heart sister and teacher from New York City; Molly Rush, mother and founder of the Thomas Merton Center in Pittsburgh and John Schuchardt, ex-marine, lawyer, father and member of Jonah House, entered the General Electric Nuclear Missile Re-entry Division in King of Prussia, PA where nose cones for the Mark 12A warheads were made.

They hammered on two nose cones, poured blood on documents and offered prayers for peace. They were arrested and initially charged with over ten different felony and misdemeanor counts. In February 1981, they underwent a jury trial in Norristown, Pennsylvania. During their trial they were denied a "justification defense" and could not present expert testimony. Due to the Court's suppression of individual testimony about the Mark 12A and U.S. nuclear war-fighting policies, four left the trial and returned to witness at G.E. They were re-arrested and returned to court. They were convicted by a jury of burglary, conspiracy and criminal mischief and sentenced to prison terms of five to ten years. They appealed and the Pennsylvania Superior Court reversed their conviction in February 1984. The State of Pennsylvania then appealed that decision.

Following a ruling in the fall of 1985 by the Pennsylvania Supreme Court in favor of the State on certain issues (including the exclusion of the justification defense), the case was returned to the Superior Court Appeals Panel. In December of 1987, the Superior Court of Pennsylvania refused their appeal, but ordered a re-sentencing. This ruling, however, was appealed to the Pennsylvania Supreme Court. In February 1989, the Pennsylvania Supreme Court denied a hearing of any further issues in the case, and on October 2, 1989 the U.S. Supreme Court announced it would not hear the Plowshares Eight Appeal.

On April 10, 1990 the Plowshares Eight were resentenced by the Pennsylvania Court of Common Pleas in Norristown and, with neither the prosecutor nor G.E. making any recommendations or asking reparations, paroled for up to 23½ months in consideration of time already served in prison. Judge James Buckingham listened attentively to statements by defendants, attorney Ramsey Clark, Dr. Robert J. Lifton, and Professors Richard Falk and Howard Zinn, placing the "crime" in the context of the common plight of humanity, international law, America's long tradition of dissent, and the primacy of individual conscience over entrenched political systems.

PLOWSHARES NUMBER TWO: On December 13, 1980 Peter DeMott, former seminarian and Vietnam veteran from Jonah House, entered the General Dynamics Electric Boat (EB) shipyard in Groton, Connecticut during the launch ceremony for the USS Baltimore fast attack submarine. Noticing an empty EB security van with keys in it, he got into the van and repeatedly rammed the Trident USS Florida denting the rudder. Security guards then broke into the van and arrested him. He was tried by a jury in New London Superior Court and convicted of criminal mischief and criminal trespass. He was sentenced to one year in jail.

THE G.E. 5: On the morning of October 29, 1981, 5 religious peace activists entered the General Electric Re-Entry Division Headquarters in Philadelphia to bring a prayer of "stop" to nuclear war preparation. The five activists were Bob Smith, Thelma Stout, Janice Hill, Roger Ludwig, and Bill Hartman. They all walked peacefully into the GE facility at 32nd & Chestnut Streets and proceeded as far as they could walk into the highly restricted area of the Advanced Engineering Laboratory. They were stopped by the coded security lock on the door; they proceeded to pour their blood onto and underneath the locked door and then knelt in prayer. They prayed for several minutes until they were taken into custody by GE security holding loaded handguns, which were placed at the heads of several members of the plowshare action.

The five activists were arrested by the Philadelphia police department and charged with Burglary [felony], Criminal Conspiracy [felony], Criminal Mischief [misdemeanor], Defiant Trespass [misdemeanor], and Criminal Trespass [felony]. All members of the witness for peace were facing 52 years under the state penal code.

A brief synopsis of the GE Five statement read as follows: "We bring our blood and hammers into this corporate house of death. Our blood speaks of the consequences of Mark 12A production - the slaughter of human life and spirit and the neglect of human needs in favor of weapons... We act today in hope with the belief that Mark12A's can be stopped, that disarmament can happen and that human beings can make peace."

On March 15, 1982 they appeared in Superior Court in Philadelphia and, to their great surprise, the charges against them were dismissed.

TRIDENT NEIN: (German for No): Independence Day, 1982, Judy Beaumont, a Benedictine sister and teacher from Chicago; Anne Montgomery, of the Plowshares Eight; James Cunningham, an ex-lawyer from Jonah House; George Veasey, a Vietnam Veteran also from Jonah House; Tim Quinn, expectant father and housepainter from Hartford, CT; Anne Bennis, teacher from Philadelphia; Bill Hartman, peace worker from Philadelphia; Vincent Kay, housepainter and poet from New Haven; and Art Laffin, member of the Covenant Peace Community in New Haven; entered EB to make a "declaration

of independence" from the Trident submarine and all nuclear weapons.

Four boarded the Trident USS Florida by canoe, hammered on several missile hatches, poured blood, and with spray paint, renamed the submarine "USS Auschwitz." They were arrested within half an hour. Meanwhile, five others entered EB's south storage yard and hammered and poured blood on two Trident sonar spheres. They were apprehended after three hours. During their two week jury trial in New London Superior Court, they were disallowed a justification defense and expert witnesses were prohibited from testifying about the dangers of the first-strike Trident. They were convicted of criminal mischief, conspiracy and criminal trespass and ordered to pay $1,386.67 in restitution to the Navy. They were sentenced to jail for up to one year.

THE PLOWSHARES CHRONOLOGY 1980-2003

PLOWSHARES NUMBER FOUR: November 14, 1982 - five days after the Trident Nein sentencing--John Grady, auto mechanic from Ithaca, New York; Ellen Grady, aide to an elderly woman and peace worker, also from Ithaca; Peter DeMott, of Plowshares Number Two; Jean Holladay, grandmother and nurse from Massachusetts; Roger Ludwig, a poet and musician involved in work with the poor in Washington, D.C.; Elmer Maas, of the Plowshares Eight; and Marcia Timmel, from the Dorothy Day Catholic Worker in Washington, D.C.; entered EB. Three boarded the Trident USS Georgia and hammered and poured blood on several missile hatches.

Four others entered the south storage yard and poured blood and hammered on Trident components before being quickly apprehended. Like the Trident Nein, they underwent a jury trial and were denied a justification defense. They also were convicted of criminal mischief, conspiracy and criminal trespass. They received prison sentences ranging from two months to one year.

AVCO PLOWSHARES: July 14, 1983 Agnes Bauerlein, mother and grandmother from Ambler, PA; Macy Morse, mother and grandmother from Nashua, NH; Mary Lyons, mother, grandmother and teacher from Hartford, CT; Frank Panopoulos, member of the Cor Jesuit community from New York City; Jean Holladay, of the Plowshares Number Four; John Pendleton, member of Jonah House; and John Schuchardt, of the Plowshares Eight; entered the AVCO Systems Division in Wilmington, Massachusetts, where MX and Pershing II nuclear weapons components are produced. They hammered on computer equipment related to these weapons systems and poured blood on blueprints labeled MX-"Peacekeeper."

THE PLOWSHARES CHRONOLOGY 1980-2003

They also issued an indictment against AVCO and its co-conspirators, including the "national security state" and the Armed Forces, for committing crimes against God and humanity by manufacturing for profit weapons of genocide. They were apprehended within an hour. During their jury trial they were able to present a justification defense but this defense and expert testimony was disallowed by the judge prior to jury deliberation. They were convicted of wanton destruction and trespass. They were sentenced to jail for up to three and one-half months. After seven years in the Massachusetts Appellate Courts, their appeal was denied on November 16, 1990. They were then sentenced to time already served which included three months for Jean and John Pendleton and nearly two weeks for the others.

GRIFFISS PLOWSHARES: On Thanksgiving Day, November 24, 1983 Jackie Allen, a nursery school teacher from Hartford, CT; Clare Grady, an artist and potter from Ithaca, NY; Dean Hammer, father and member of the Plowshares Eight; Elizabeth McAlister, mother and co-founder of Jonah House; Vern Rossman, minister, father and grandfather from Boston, MA; Kathleen Rumpf, a Catholic Worker from Marlboro, NY; and Karl Smith, member of Jonah House; entered Griffiss Air Force Base in Rome, NY. They hammered and poured blood on a B-52 bomber converted to carry cruise missiles as well as on B-52 engines. They also left at the site of their witness a written indictment of Griffiss Air Force Base and the U.S. Government

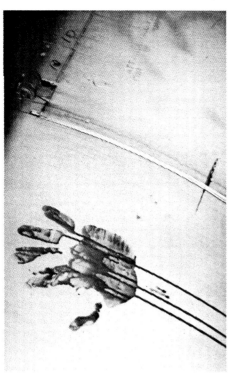

pointing to the war crimes of preparing for nuclear war and depicting how the new state religion of "nuclearism" denies constitutional rights and punishes acts of conscience. Unnoticed for several hours, they finally approached security guards and were arrested. In this, the first Plowshares case to be tried in Federal Court, their justification defense was denied. They were acquitted by a jury of sabotage, but they were convicted of conspiracy and destruction of government property. They received prison sentences ranging from two to three years. Their appeal was denied in Federal Court in March 1985.

SCHWAEBISCH-GMUEND PLOWSHARES: On December 4, 1983 Carl Kabat, of the Plowshares Eight, and three West Germans - Herwig Jantschik, Dr. Wolfgang Sternstein and Karin Vix - entered a U.S. Army base in Schwaebisch-Gmuend, West Germany and carried out the first Plowshares action in Europe. Six weeks earlier, they publicly announced their actions, but did not disclose the exact date or place. They participated in a six-week peace march where they distributed a booklet informing the public and media about their action and previous plowshares actions. On December 4, they entered the base early in the morning and with hammers and bolt cutters disarmed a Pershing II missile launcher. They were soon apprehended by U.S. soldiers. Following their arrest, they were all released on personal recognizance. Carl returned to the U.S. and did not attend the trial. During the first week of February 1985, the three Germans were tried before the three judges and two lay judges and convicted. After their conviction, the judges called the Pershing II a "bad prophesy," and characterized their action as violence. Herwig and Wolfgang were sentenced to 1800 DM ($900) or 90 days in jail, while Karin was sentenced to 450 dm ($225) or 60 days in jail. Karin and Herwig served their prison sentence; Wolfgang paid the fine.

THE PLOWSHARES CHRONOLOGY 1980-2003

PERSHING PLOWSHARES: In the season of Passover, Easter Morning, April 22, 1984 Per Herngren, a student and peace worker from Sweden; Paul Magno, from the Dorothy Day Catholic Worker in Washington, D.C.; Todd Kaplan, involved in work with the poor in Washington, D.C.; Tim Lietzke, member of Jeremiah House in Richmond, VA; Anne Montgomery, of the Plowshares Eight and Trident Nein; Patrick O'Neill, university student and peace worker from Greenville, North Carolina; Jim Perkins, teacher, father and member of Jonah House; and Christin Schmidt, university student and peace worker from Rhode Island; entered Martin Marietta in Orlando, Florida. Once inside, they hammered and poured blood on Pershing II missile components and on a Patriot missile launcher. They also served Martin Marietta with an indictment for engaging in the criminal activity of building nuclear weapons in violation of Divine, international and national law. They also displayed a banner which said: "Violence Ends Where Love Begins." They were apprehended after several hours.

During their jury trial in Federal Court they were denied a justification defense. They were convicted of depredation of government property and conspiracy. They were sentenced to three years in federal prison, given five year suspended sentences with probation, and each ordered to pay $2,900 in restitution. Both their appeal and motion for reduction of sentence were denied in Federal

THE PLOWSHARES CHRONOLOGY 1980-2003

Court. Herngren, a Swedish national, was deported on August 27, 1985 after serving over a year of his sentence.

SPERRY SOFTWARE PAIR: August 10, 1984 John LaForge and Barbara Katt, house painters and peace workers from Bemidji, MN, dressed as quality control inspectors, entered Sperry Corporation in Eagan, Minnesota. Once inside they poured blood and hammered on two prototype computers designed to provide guidance and navigation information for Trident submarines and F4G fighter-bombers. In addressing Sperry's nuclear war preparations, they also served Sperry with a citizens indictment declaring that they are committing war crimes in violation of national and international law. After a two-day jury trial in Federal Court in which they were allowed to present a justification defense, they were convicted of destruction of government property. Judge Miles Lord imposed a six month suspended sentence and used the occasion to criticize the arms industry, and to cite Sperry's corporate corruption. He also recognized the legitimacy of the justification defense for civil disobedience trials and for the Sperry Software trial in particular.

TRIDENT II PLOWSHARES: October 1, 1984 William Boston, a house painter and peace worker from New Haven, CT; Jean Holladay, of the Plowshares Number Four and AVCO Plowshares; Frank Panopoulos and John Pendleton of the AVCO Plowshares; and Leo Schiff, draft registration resister and natural foods chef from

Vermont; entered the EB Quonset Point facility in North Kingston, Rhode Island. They hammered and poured blood on six Trident II missile tubes and unfurled a banner which said: "Harvest of Hope - Swords into Plowshares." They also placed a pumpkin at the site and posted a written "Call to Conscience" on the missile tubes condemning these weapons under international and religious law and calling on those responsible to cease their crimes against humanity. They were arrested within half an hour and charged with possession of burglary tools, malicious damage to property and criminal trespass. During their jury trial, expert witnesses were allowed to be qualified in the presence of the jury. However the judge ruled this and other expert testimony irrelevant and denied a justification defense. At the end of their two weeklong trials, the prosecution dropped the burglary tools charge (a felony carrying ten years) as the defendants pled guilty to the malicious damage to property charge. (After the State's case, the judge dismissed the trespass charge). After two days of prayer and discernment, the five concluded that pleading guilty was the most nonviolent course to take. On October 18, 1985 they were each sentenced to one year and a $500 fine. Frank was given an additional two months for a contempt charge relating to his refusal to disclose to the judge who drove the group to EB.

SILO PRUNING HOOKS: November 12, 1984 Carl Kabat, of the Plowshares Eight and Plowshares Number Seven; Paul Kabat, an Oblate priest from Minnesota; Larry Cloud Morgan, Native American and mental health care worker from Minneapolis, MN; Helen Woodson, mother of eleven children and founder of the Gaudete

THE PLOWSHARES CHRONOLOGY 1980-2003

Peace and Justice Center from Madison, WI; entered a Minuteman II missile silo controlled by Whiteman Air Force Base in Knob Noster, Missouri. Once inside the silo area, they used a jackhammer and air compressor to damage the silo cover lid. They then offered a Eucharist and left at the silo a Biblical and Native American indictment of the U.S. government and the institutional church for their complicity in the pending omnicide of nuclear holocaust. They were arrested close to an hour after their action by armed military guards authorized to use "deadly force" against intruders. Following their arrest, they were declared by the court to be a "threat to the community" and were thus held on "preventive detention" and denied bond.

They underwent a jury trial in Federal Court in February 1985 in Kansas City, Missouri. They were convicted of destruction of government property, conspiracy, intent to damage the national defense and trespass. On March 27, 1985 they received the most severe prison sentences to date of any Plowshares group: Larry--eight years; Paul--ten years; and Carl and Helen--eighteen years.

THE PLOWSHARES CHRONOLOGY 1980-2003
[23]

They were also given three to five years probation and ordered to pay $2,932.80 each in restitution. On November 1, 1985 U.S. District Judge D. Brook Bartlett, their trial judge, reduced Helen's sentence from eighteen to twelve years, including 5 years probation. In March 1987, Larry and Paul were released from prison following a sentence reduction hearing. Larry's sentence was reduced to 36 months and three years probation while Paul's sentence was reduced to 40 months and 4 years probation. Both were required to perform 300 hours of community service and not violate the law for the duration of their probation. All but Helen appealed. Their appeals were denied in the spring of 1986.

On April 22, 1987 the U.S. Supreme Court ruled not to consider Carl's appeal. His sentence was reduced to 10 years including 5 years probation. On April 12, 1991 Carl was released on probation with the condition that he pay restitution. For reasons of conscience he has refused to comply with this order. On January 27, 1989 Larry was convicted of two counts of going out of the district of Minnesota, a violation of his probation, and was sentenced to prison for one year. The occasions of his departures were to attend protests at the Trident base in King's Bay Georgia. He was taken into custody by U.S. marshals at a church near the Trident base. Due to health reasons the Judge recommended that Larry be sent to the Medical Center for Federal Prisoners in Rochester, Minnesota. Larry was released on November 13, 1989.

RESISTANCE IN CAPTIVITY - On March 16, 1988 Helen Woodson walked through the main gate of Alderson Prison carrying a banner and statement protesting the nuclear arms race, pollution of the environment and prison conditions for women. She was apprehended outside the prison by a patrol vehicle. She was temporarily placed in solitary confinement and then transferred to FCI Pleasanton in California. On December 10, 1988 in honor of Gaudete (Rejoice!) Sunday, Helen carried out another resistance action, this time, at FCI Pleasanton. She walked to the rec field track bearing an athletic bag stuffed with sheets, towels and papers doused with flammable nail polish, set the bag next to the fence and ignited a "lovely Advent blaze." Then she hung a banner reading: "There is no security in the U.S. government, nuclear weapons, chemical contaminants, prisons and UNICOR-military prison industries. Fences make slaves. Tear Them Down." And then, with toenail clippers, she snipped the "security" alarm wire, severing it in four separate places.

She was sent to the hole and charged with attempted escape, arson, destruction of government property and inciting to riot. In late January 1989 she was moved to MCC San Diego. Before leaving Pleasanton she learned that the evidence for her action was destroyed and she was not prosecuted. After a short stint in San Diego, she was transferred to Marianna Prison in Florida. As a result of federal appeals court ruling, Helen was released on parole on June 14, 1993. During the spring of 1993 an appeals court overturned a lower court ruling and affirmed the government's position that it could release Helen on parole. Helen had filed a civil suit asking to be held in prison until the expiration of her sentence, and then be unconditionally released. Three days after her release, she was involved in several controversial protests (which went outside the bounds of traditional nonviolent protest) focusing on the idolatry of money, corporate greed and the destruction of the earth. She was arrested and convicted for these actions and was sentenced to 202 months in prison.

MINUTEMAN II PLOWSHARES: February 19, 1985 Martin Holladay, a carpenter from Sheffield, Vermont, entered another Minuteman II missile silo of Whiteman Air Force Base near Odessa, Missouri. With hammer and chisel, he damaged the silo lid and some electrical boxes. He also poured blood on the silo and spray-painted "No More Hiroshimas." He left at the site an indictment charging the U.S. government with committing crimes against God and international law by its nuclear war preparations. After his arrest, he was denied bond and held until trial. During his four-day jury trial, he was denied the opportunity to present a justification defense. On April 25, 1985 he was convicted of destruction of government property and destruction of national defense material. He was sentenced on May 16, 1985, to eight years in federal prison and five years probation. He was also fined $1,000 and ordered to pay $2,242 in restitution. Martin was released from prison after 19 months following a sentence reduction hearing on September 24, 1986. He remained on probation through 1991 and was required to pay restitution.

TRIDENT II PRUNING HOOKS: April 18, 1985 Greg Boertje, ex-army officer and peace organizer from Louisiana; John Heid, former Franciscan seminarian and social worker from Ithaca, NY; Roger Ludwig, of the Plowshares Number Four; Sheila Parks, former college teacher from Medford, MA; Suzanne Schmidt, mother, grandmother, worker with the disabled and member of Jonah House; and George Veasey, of the Trident Nein; entered the EB Quonset Point facility in North Kingston, Rhode Island - the same site where the Trident II Plowshares had acted seven months earlier. They poured blood and hammered on three Trident II missile tubes and spray-painted "Dachau" on them. They left there a "Call to Conscience" indicting General Dynamics for war crimes and preparing for a war of aggression in violation of international, constitutional and spiritual law. Arrested after a short time, they were charged with possession of burglary tools, malicious damage to property and criminal trespass. While Sheila and Suzanne were released nearly a month after the action on a "promise to appear" (PTA) and John after five months, Greg, George and Roger remained in jail for nearly nine months, refusing to accept a PTA for reasons of conscience. Shortly before their trial date, the judge released the three unconditionally from prison. During their two-week jury trial, the judge denied their justification defense, insisting that their motives were irrelevant to the case. They were convicted of all three charges. In a special gesture of support for the group, four jurors had the judge publicly read a statement from them conveying that they were sympathetic to their cause. On March 31, 1986 they were sentenced to three years, suspended after one year, and given three years probation which involved various levels of non-cooperation by the group. John, Greg, George and Roger were released during the summer of 1986. Sheila and Suzanne were released in January 1987.

MICHIGAN ELF DISARMAMENT ACTION: May 28, 1985 Tom Hastings, a Wisconsin peace activist involved in radio work, entered a wooded area in Michigan's upper peninsula and sawed down one of the poles carrying the Navy's "Extremely Low Frequency" (ELF) transmitter antennas which are used to coordinate the communications, command, and control process of all nuclear submarines in the U.S. He remained at the site for 45 minutes, praying, singing and planting a circle of corn around the pole. The next morning, he gave a part of the pole to Congressman Bob Davis' office and turned himself in to the local sheriff. Held for 48 hours, he was released on personal recognizance. He underwent a jury trial and was convicted of malicious destruction of property. On September 27, 1985 he was sentenced to fifteen days and two years probation.

PANTEX DISARMAMENT ACTION: July 16, 1985, Richard Miller, involved in work with the poor in Des Moines, Iowa, began dismantling a section of railroad track from the railroad spur leading from U.S. Department of Energy's Pantex Nuclear Weapons Assembly Plant in Amarillo, Texas to a main line of the Topeka and Santa Fe Railroad. After first taking extensive precautions to prevent accidental derailment and avoid personal injury, he labored with railroad tools for seven hours, removing a 39-foot section of rail. Pointing out the connection between the Nazi extermination camp at Auschwitz and the Pantex factory, which is the final assembly point for every nuclear weapon made in the U.S., he put up a banner that read: "Pantex=Auschwitz - Stop the Trains." He further stated: "At Auschwitz the trains carried the people to the crematoria; at Pantex the trains carry the crematoria to the people." Charged with "wrecking trains" and destruction of national defense materials, he underwent a jury trial in Federal Court and was convicted. On November 8, 1985 he was sentenced to two four-year sentences to run concurrently. He was released from prison in February 1989 upon completing his sentence.

WISCONSIN ELF DISARMAMENT ACTION: August 14, 1985 Jeff Leys, a draft registration resister and peace worker from St. Paul, Minnesota, continued the process of disarming ELF (see Michigan ELF action) by sawing two deep notches in an ELF pole hoping to weaken it and leaving the rest to natural forces. (Unlike the Michigan ELF still under construction, the 56-mile Wisconsin ELF system is fully operational, with 1.5 million watts flowing through it). In a statement he carried with him to the site he explained: "I act today in accordance with the teachings of Gandhi, Christ and the Indians - and in accordance with the basic underpinnings of humanity, as expressed in the various world religions and international laws." After an hour, Jeff walked to a transmitter site to turn himself in. Jailed after his arrest, he was tried by a jury on September 30, 1985 and was convicted of criminal damage to property. On October 29, 1985 Jeff was sentenced to five months in jail and given a three year suspended sentence with three years probation. He was also ordered to pay $4,775 in restitution. In April of 1986 Jeff began serving his three-year sentence because of his refusal to pay restitution for reasons of conscience. His appeal was denied in September 1986. He was released in August 1987.

MARTIN MARIETTA MX WITNESS: September 27, 1985 Al Zook, father and grandfather active with the Catholic Worker in Denver, CO; Mary Sprunger-Froese, member of the Bijou Community and involved in hospitality work in Colorado Springs, CO; and Marie Nord, a Minnesota Franciscan sister involved in hospitality work for women; entered Martin Marietta's Denver, Colorado plant. (Martin Marietta has a $2 billion contract for building and testing the MX missile). With the intent of disarming components of the MX missile, they carried blood and hammers into the MX work area. Finding the area highly secured by employees wearing "peacekeeper" security badges, the three were not able to enter areas where MX work is done and directly disarm any MX components. They were, however, able to pour blood on large interior windows overlooking the work areas and unfurled their banner: "Swords Into Plowshares." They were quickly arrested and each charged with felony burglary and criminal mischief. The burglary charge was eventually dropped, however the criminal mischief charge was changed from a misdemeanor to a felony. They were imprisoned for one month before they were released on their own recognizance. On March 5, 1986 they were found guilty by a jury of criminal mischief exceeding $300. During their trial the judge refused to hear their justification defense. On May 1, 1986 they were sentenced to two months in prison. Al and Marie appealed their case and the Colorado Court of Appeals reversed their convictions. The appeal was based on the judge's denial of their motion to proceed in forma pauperis, after his determination that their indigency was voluntary. The state had petitioned for a review of the case before deciding not to retry Al and Marie.

SILO PLOWSHARES: Good Friday, March 28, 1986 Darla Bradley and Larry Morlan of the Davenport Catholic Worker in Iowa; Jean Gump, a mother of twelve and grandmother from Morton Grove, Illinois; Ken Rippetoe, a member of the Catholic Worker in Rock Island, Illinois; and John Volpe, father, former employee at the Rock Island Arsenal and member of the Davenport Catholic Worker; entered two Minuteman Missile Silos controlled by Whiteman Air Force Base near Holden, Missouri. Dividing into two groups, the first group of three went to Silo M10 while the second group went to Silo M6. Hanging banners on the silo fences, one of which read: "Disarmament - An Act of Healing" they employed sledgehammers to split and disarm the geared central track used to move the 120 ton missile silo cover at the time of launch. They also cut circuits and used masonry hammers to damage electrical sensor equipment. They then poured blood on the silo covers in the form of a cross and spray-painted "Disarm and Live" and "For the Children" on the silo pad. They left at the site an indictment charging the U.S. government with committing crimes against the laws of God and humanity and indicting as well the institutional Christian church for its complicity in the arms race. They were arrested nearly 40 minutes after their action by heavily armed military police. Following their arrest they were taken into custody and then released on their own recognizance. During their five-day jury trial they presented important evidence regarding their state of mind but the jury was not allowed to consider justification as a defense. On June 27, 1986 they were convicted of destruction of government property and conspiracy. In addition, Jean, Larry and Darla were cited for contempt for refusing to answer questions about where they met prior to the action.

They served seven days in jail following the trial. John and Ken were also imprisoned for refusing to cooperate with the conditions of their release so long as the others were imprisoned for contempt. They were released on July 8. On August 22, 1986 Darla, Jean, Ken and Larry were sentenced to 8 years with 5 years probation while John was sentenced to 7 years with 5 years probation. John and Darla were ordered to pay $1,680 in restitution while Larry, Jean and Ken were ordered to pay $424. Each was also fined $100. In April 1987, John was released from prison following a sentence reduction hearing. His sentence was reduced to 10 months, 5 years probation, and was required to pay restitution. Ken and Darla were released from prison in mid-June 1987 after their sentence was reduced to one year. They were placed on probation for 5 years and were ordered to pay restitution. On April 18, 1990 his $424 having been paid anonymously, Larry, who had been imprisoned since his action, went to a halfway house and was released on probation on July 20, 1990. And in October of 1990, after four years of imprisonment, Jean was released on probation.

PERSHING TO PLOWSHARES: On December 12, 1986 on the 7th anniversary of the NATO decision to deploy the Cruise and the Pershing II missles in Europe, Heike Huschauer, a city council member of Neuss, West Germany; Suzanne Mauch-Fritz, a social worker from Stuttgart; Wolfgang Sternstein, Plowshares activist; and Stellan Vinthagen, an orderly from Sweden; entered a back-up U.S. Army weapons depot at Schwabisch-Gmund, West Germany and damaged the tractor-rig of a Pershing II Missile Launch box. They hammered on the crane that maneuvers the missile and on the generator that operates the launcher, and poured blood on the rig.

The banner which they hung over the truck stated, "Choose Life for the Children and Poor." These words were also spray painted on the roadway. They were discovered after thirty minutes, when they signaled to a nearby guard. In a statement of intent the four said, "With awareness of our responsibility we understand that we are the ones who make the arms race possible by not trying to stop it."

Following their arrest, they were released. On October 11 through October 19, 1989 nearly three years after their disarmament action, they were tried before three professional judges and three lay judges on the charges of sabotage, damage to government property and trespassing. During their trial they were allowed to present evidence about the moral and legal justification for their action. They pleaded that if the court accepts their justification defense they must be acquitted. If not, they must be given a high sentence. The court did not accept their pleading and were given the following sentences: Wolfgang 1200 DM or 120 days in jail, Heike, Suzanne and Stellan 600 DM or 60 days in jail. In addition, for a subsequent blockade action, Stellan, Heike and Wolfgang were sentenced to 20, 80 and 135 days, respectively. Suzanne paid the 600 DM fine. Stellen and Wolfgang served their sentences and were released in April 1990. On March 4, 1991 Heike was ordered to serve her 101-day sentence despite her appeal for a postponement of sentence so that she could continue her organizing efforts to end the U.S. war against Iraq.

EPIPHANY PLOWSHARES: On January 6, 1987 the Christian Feast of Epiphany, Greg Boertje, of the Trident II Pruning Hooks; Rev.

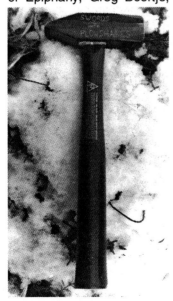

Dexter Lanctot and Rev. Thomas McGann, priests of the Archdiocese of Philadelphia; and Lin Romano, an advocate for the poor from Washington, D.C.; entered the Willow Grove Naval Air Station in Horsham, PA. Dividing into two groups, one group went to a Navy P-3 Orion anti-submarine aircraft - an essential part of the U.S. first-strike arsenal. Meanwhile the other group went to a Marine CH-53 Sea Stallion and an Army H-1 Huey helicopter - both integral parts of U.S. interventionary forces. Both groups hammered and poured blood on the aircraft and displayed banners which proclaimed: "Seek the Disarmed Christ" and "Espadas en Arados - Swords into Plowshares." The four left behind a statement which explained why they acted on Epiphany, the Christian feast that recalls the 3 Magis' search for the Christ child, "who came in the name of Peace." Having therefore addressed the "deadly connection" between nuclear weapons and military intervention, they also left an indictment of the U.S. government for its criminal interventionary wars in Central America and the Middle East and its first-strike nuclear war-making policies. They were charged with conspiracy, destruction of government property and trespass - charges which carry up to 15½ years. On March 31, they underwent a weeklong jury trial in Federal Court in Philadelphia and were prevented from presenting a crime prevention or necessity defense.

For the first time in a Plowshares case, the trial ended in a hung jury and a mistrial. On May 11, 1987 they were retried. The defendants were once again denied their affirmative defenses and their testimony was even more severely restricted than in the first trial. Despite the constraints of the court, their trial once again ended in a hung jury and a mistrial. In an interview following the trial, one juror stated he believed the group did not act with criminal intent and affirmed their efforts for disarmament. After the second trial the two priests, who were suspended from their priestly duties after the action, accepted a plea bargain, pled guilty to criminal trespass, and were sentenced to 100 days in federal prison plus $500 fines. Their suspensions were lifted following their release from prison. On July

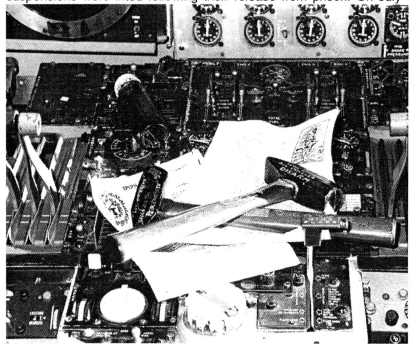

THE PLOWSHARES CHRONOLOGY 1980-2003

13, 1987 a third trial began for Boertje and Romano. This trial ended in a mistrial when the judge ruled that the jury had been "contaminated" by statements from the defendants and spectators on such forbidden topics as international law. On September 21, 1987 a fourth trial began, with the judge's repressive "gag order" remaining in effect. During the trial, both defendants received two contempt charges and had lawyers appointed to represent them (defendants had been representing themselves).

On September 25, 1987 they were found guilty of all three charges. On November 17, Lin was sentenced to 2 years and 100 days in prison plus 5 years probation. For reasons of conscience, Greg chose not to appear for sentencing. In a written public statement issued at the time of sentencing, Greg stated his intention to go "underground" and eventually emerge in another non-violent action. Following his trial, conviction and sentencing for the Nuclear Navy Plowshares action, Greg was sentenced to 33 months for failing to appear at the original sentencing for the Epiphany action. Lin, and then Greg, appealed their case from prison on the grounds that the judge violated their "pro se" rights when he appointed lawyers to represent them. They won the appeal and each was granted individual trials. Lin was eventually released from prison after serving nine months. In November 1988 her charges were reduced to trespass, whereby she was not entitled to a jury trial. She was tried before a U.S. Magistrate, convicted, and was sentenced to two years probation even though she had already served more jail time than the maximum sentence for trespass--six months. In April 1989 charges against Greg were dropped, though he still had to serve a 33-month sentence for failure to appear at sentencing. In July 1990, Greg was released from prison and placed on probation.

PAUPERS PLOWSHARES: On Good Friday, April 17, 1987 two brothers, Fr. Pat Sieber, a Franciscan priest working at St. Francis Inn, a shelter for the homeless and soup kitchen in Philadelphia; and Rick Sieber, a father of three also working at St. Francis Inn; entered the Naval Air Development Center in Warminster, PA. Once inside they dug a hole and buried a foot-long coffin that listed the names of 65 homeless and poor people who have been buried in an unkept lot in northeast Philadelphia known since 1980 as potter's or "pauper's" field. They also placed a 3-foot cross bearing the same names on top of the makeshift grave.

They then approached a P-3 Orion aircraft - an integral part of the U.S. first-strike arsenal - and hammered on the plane's strobe light, cut wires in the nose of the plane and poured blood on a wing and fuselage area of the aircraft. While awaiting arrest they knelt in prayer and held a banner which said: "God Hears the Cry of the

Poor." They left at the site a statement and indictment addressing the criminality of U.S. nuclear war preparations, the priority the government gives to arms over the poor, and how these arms preparations are actually killing the poor. In addition to signing their own names to these statements, they also signed the name "Lazarus" to represent the poor for whom they acted. They were arrested after a half an hour and charged with unlawful entry and destruction of

government property. On June 12, the charges were reduced to one misdemeanor --unlawful entry. On August 5, 1987 after an hour-long bench trial, the pair were found guilty of unlawful entry. They were sentenced to one year's probation, fined $100 and ordered to pay $1,540 in restitution. In February 1989 their restitution was dropped and they paid their fine which went towards a victims' compensation fund.

WHITE ROSE DISARMAMENT ACTION: On June 2, 1987 in the early morning, Katya Komisaruk, a peace activist from the San Francisco Bay area, walked through an unlocked gate leaving cookies and a bouquet of flowers for security guards and entered a satellite control facility named NAVSTAR at the Vandenberg AFB in Santa Barbara County, California. (NAVSTAR is the U.S. global positioning system of satellites. When fully operational, this system will consist of 18 orbiting satellites which will be able to provide the navigational and guidance signals to Trident II and other nuclear missiles as well as the Star Wars system, for a first-strike nuclear attack.) Once inside, she used a hammer, crowbar and cordless electric drill to damage panels of an IBM mainframe computer and a satellite dish on top of the building. Using a crowbar she removed the computer's chipboards and danced on them. On the walls she spray-painted "Nuremberg," "International Law," and statements for disarmament. After being undetected for two hours, she left the base and hitchhiked to San Francisco. The next morning she held a press conference at the Federal Building in San Francisco to explain her action whereupon she was taken into custody by the FBI.

She was charged with sabotage and destruction of government property. Each charge carries a maximum penalty of ten years in prison and/or a $250,000 fine. The day before her trial the sabotage charge was dropped in the face of a defense brief that had been earlier submitted calling upon the government to prove every element of the charge beyond a reasonable doubt. Her trial began on November 10, 1987 in Los Angeles Federal Court. Several weeks before the trial, Judge Rea ruled in favor of the U.S. prosecutor's "motion in limine" which would severely restrict the evidence allowed as well as Katya's personal testimony. Katya, who represented herself and was assisted by co-counsel, was not allowed to mention words like "nuclear missiles" or "first-strike." The jury found her guilty of destruction of property on November 16, 1987. On January 11, 1988 Katya was sentenced to 5 years in prison. In addition Judge Rea ordered her to pay $500,000 restitution because he had heard that there might be a movie or book based on her action. Katya closely identifies with Sophie Scholl, a young German woman and member of the White Rose group during World War II, who was executed by the Third Reich for publicly opposing Nazi atrocities. On February 9, 1990 Katya was released from prison and placed on probation for the duration of her 5-year sentence.

TRANSFIGURATION PLOWSHARES (WEST): On August 5, 1987 at 5:15 p.m., the exact moment (8:15 a.m. in Japan) when the U.S. dropped the first atomic bomb on Hiroshima in 1945, Jerry Ebner, a member of the Catholic Worker Community of Milwaukee; Joe Gump, father of twelve and husband of the imprisoned Jean Gump of the Silo Plowshares from Morton Grove, Ill.; and Helen Woodson, acting as a "co-conspirator" from Shakopee Prison in Minnesota where she was serving a 17 year sentence for the Silo Pruning Hooks action, carried out the fourth non-violent disarmament of a minuteman missile silo controlled by Whiteman AFB in Missouri. They went to silo K-9 near Butler, Mo., and once inside the silo area, Jerry and Joe locked themselves within the fenced in area with a kryptonite bicycle lock. After pouring their own blood in the shape of a cross on the concrete silo lid, they used one eight and one three pound sledgehammer on the tracks used to open the silo lid. They also hammered on electrical connectors and other apparatus and cut various electric wires with bolt cutters. They then hung disarmament banners and sang and prayed while awaiting arrest. They also left at the site their action statement and indictment, signed by the three, as well as a photo of Jerry, Joe and Helen. In the interest of 'conservation' they used the very same banners and bolt cutters used by the Silo Pruning Hooks and Silo Plowshares. A while later military police arrived in a vehicle armed with a machine gun and arrested Jerry and Joe.

Explaining her involvement in the action, Helen stated she participated "in spirit" through a "conspiracy for life." The three named themselves the "Transfiguration Plowshares" to commemorate the Transfiguration, the Christian feast celebrated on August 6 which recalls the revelation of Christ to his disciples as the Lord of heaven and earth and also represents a foreshadowing of Christ's resurrection. At a mid-August court hearing they were charged with a two count felony indictment: conspiring to damage government property and destruction of government property - both federal charges. In a relatively open trial, the two were allowed to show a video film entitled "Hiroshima/Nagasaki: 1945." This video, which the two carried into the silo with them, contained footage of the immediate effect of the bomb dropped on the two cities. Jerry was able to sing two songs to the jury which he first sang at the silo. Judge Howard Sachs, however, made it clear in his instructions to the jury that these things were ultimately irrelevant to the case before them. On October 22, the jury found them guilty. On December 11, 1987 Jerry Ebner and Joe Gump were sentenced to 40 and 30 months respectively in prison. Joe was released in November 1989. Jerry served more than two years in prison before being paroled. After being out of prison for a period of time he was jailed once again during the summer of 1990 for not cooperating with the conditions of his parole. He was released from federal prison on April 5, 1991 and remained on probation through 1994.

TRANSFIGURATION PLOWSHARES (EAST): On August 6, 1987, Hiroshima Day and the Christian feast of the Transfiguration, Margaret Brodhead, a journalist; Dan Ethier, a former computer programmer and Catholic Worker; and Tom Lewis, artist and long-time peace activist - all from Worcester, MA - entered the South Weymouth Naval Air Station near Boston at dawn. They hammered and poured blood on the bomb bay doors and bomb racks of a P-3 Orion nuclear-capable anti-submarine plane which can use nuclear depth charges and homing torpedoes to attack submarines. They hammered as well on the magnetic anomaly detector of an S-H 2F LAMPS MK-I Sea Sprite helicopter. (These same types of aircraft are currently deployed by U.S. forces in the Persian Gulf and are an integral part of U.S. offensive anti-submarine warfare strategy, which allows the Navy to project force in the Middle East as well as Central America). They also hung pictures of Hiroshima victims on the aircraft as well as a "Swords Into Plowshares" banner. In a signed statement and indictment they left at the site, they said "the blinding light of that first atomic bomb turned life into death, but the blinding light of the Transfiguration revealed that death would be turned into life in Christ's Resurrection." They further charged the "Nuclear National Security State" with contravening international and divine laws. They were taken into custody by base security shortly after their action as they knelt in prayer holding a banner that read "Christ Transfigured - Death Into Life."

The three were initially charged with unlawful entry, a federal misdemeanor. In December, Dan plead no contest and was sentenced to six months probation and community service of 100 hours. Tom and Meg were convicted on March 4, 1988 after a 6-hour bench trial in Boston, where they presented testimony on the unconstitutionality of the arms race and the aircraft's status as "instrumentalities of crime" under international law. On April 26, Meg and Tom were sentenced to six months probation and 100 hours community service.

HARMONIC DISARMAMENT FOR LIFE: On August 16, 1987 the day of Harmonic Convergence, George Ostensen, a peace activist from the Northeast, in conspiracy with plowshares prisoner Helen Woodson, enacted a Plowshares action at the ELF Communication System Transmitter Site near Clam Lake, Wisconsin. Early in the morning, George entered the North ground of the ELF Trident communication system. Using a hatchet, saw, and other tools, he proceeded to cut down three ELF poles, notched two other poles, and cut some ground wires. He poured blood over the poles, hammered on ground-well electrical control boxes, placed photos of children and planted flowers inside the boxes and near the poles, and hung peace banners. In statements he carried on to the site George stated: "I act at the ELF Trident communication system in an attempt to stop these deadly messages from being transmitted. These Extremely Low Frequencies hurt our earth by subjecting all God's creatures to highly unstable electromagnetic non-ionizing radiation and giving the Trident first-strike capability to destroy all life."

In reference to the Harmonic Convergence, the lining up of the planets on August 15 and 16, he stated the convergence is the beginning of the new age, the age of change, movement, spiritual consciousness, and harmony according to ancient Mayan, Tibetan and Hopi calendars. Following his action at the North Ground,

George, undetected, went to the Terminal Control Center to inform the security guards on duty of his action. After spray-painting on the Terminal Center "Trident - ELF is in violation of International Law and God's Law" and "Swords Into Plowshares" he spoke with a security guard who asked him to leave the site. George then went to a fenced in area near the control center and manually switched off several generators used to control computers and electricity at the site. George did this three times, following warnings to security personnel that the ELF site must be shut down. Finally, the local sheriff was called and George was arrested -- some nine hours after he entered the site. On August 20, George was charged with two felony counts of sabotage - both state charges and each carrying a maximum penalty of ten years in prison if convicted. The indictment also listed Helen as aiding and abetting in the action and noted the ELF site had to be closed for 29 hours. On January 10, 1988 following a three day jury trial in Ashland County District Court, George was convicted of one count of sabotage and acquitted on the second count.

On February 12, 1988 George was sentenced to 33 months. In July 1988 he was denied parole. On May 2, 1989 his appeal was denied by the Wisconsin Court of Appeals and the court ruled that his sabotage conviction was valid. He was released from prison in September 1989 after serving two-thirds of his sentence. On October 2, Gandhi's birthday, he returned to ELF with other friends and carried a Swords Into Plowshares banner up the road to the transmitter site. He was arrested and returned to jail. He waived a parole revocation hearing and was ordered to serve the remaining 11 months of his original sentence. On January 30, 1990 he was released from prison.

AUSTRALIAN PLOWSHARES ACTION: On December 28, 1987, the feast of the Holy Innocents, Marie Grunke, a Blessed Sacrament Sister of Newtown; Joanne Merrigan and Anthony Gwyther, both of the St. Francis House, Darlinghurst; boarded the USS Leftwich during a public inspection while it was anchored in Sydney Harbor. The USS Leftwich is a nuclear-capable destroyer of the Spruance class recently deployed in the Persian Gulf. Recalling the innocents that were killed by King Herod and those children that continue to die from war and hunger, they poured their own blood on an ASROC anti-submarine nuclear depth charge launcher and a Tomahawk cruise missile launcher, weapons of first-strike capability. They hammered on these weapons to begin their disarmament and initiate their conversion into instruments of peace. After leaving their action statement on the ship, they were escorted off without being arrested or charged. This was the first Australian plowshares action.

NUCLEAR NAVY PLOWSHARES: On Easter Sunday, April 3, 1988, Philip Berrigan of Jonah House (and original Plowshares 8); Andrew Lawrence of the Community for Creative Non-Violence; Sr. Margaret McKenna, a Doctor of Theology and member of the Medical Mission Sisters in Philadelphia; and Greg Boertje, former Army officer and member of Trident II Pruning Hooks and Epiphany Plowshares; boarded the battleship Iowa at Norfolk Naval Station in Virginia. The four boarded the battleship as part of a public tour greeting the vessel on its return from service in the Persian Gulf. The four disarmed two armored box launchers for the Tomahawk Cruise Missile, hammering and pouring blood, and unfurled two banners: Seek the Disarmed Christ, and Tomahawks Into Plowshares. The four worked for two or three minutes before they were seen by security. When ordered to stop they did so: a "security alert" was sounded and the pier was vacated of all but naval personnel. Hundreds of people had come on Easter Sunday to visit the USS Iowa and the USS America which was also on display. Tours of both vessels were shut down.

Andrew, Greg, Margaret and Phil were held for some time at the Naval Base, questioned by the FBI and then transported by the FBI to Virginia Beach. They appeared in court on April 4, were charged with criminal trespass - a charge which does not entitle defendants to a jury trial. Because of Greg's status as a fugitive (stemming from his non-appearance at the sentencing for the Epiphany Plowshares) he was held on $25,000 bond. Though the others were offered a personal recognizance bond, they refused this

bond as an act of solidarity with Greg. They were tried before a U.S. Magistrate on May 19, 1988 at the Norfolk Virginia Federal Court and convicted of trespass. In an effort to diffuse courtroom support, the sentencing of the 4 was set on different days during July 1989. Margaret was sentenced to time served (over 3 months), 2 years probation and 240 hours community service and prohibited from entering any military installation during her probation. She was then released. Andrew received a 4-month sentence. Greg and Phil each received the maximum sentence of 6 months. In March 1989 Margaret received a 4-month jail sentence for refusing to cooperate with the conditions of her probation. However she was credited with the time she already served before trial and ordered to jail for 20 days.

KAIROS PLOWSHARES: In the pre-dawn hours of June 26, 1988 Kathleen Maire, a Franciscan sister of Allegheny, NY; Jack Marth, a member of POTS (Part of the Solution) in the Bronx, NY; Sr. Anne Montgomery, a participant in three previous plowshares actions; and Christine Mulready, member of the Sisters of St. Joseph of Brentwood, NY; approached the Trident submarine, USS Pennsylvania at EB in Groton, CT, with the intent of carrying out a symbolic act of disarmament. Paddling against the current in the midst of a fast approaching storm, they were spotted in their rubber rafts in the Thames River by EB security before reaching the Trident.

Apprehended by EB security, they were held overnight in jail. They were arraigned on charges of trespass, conspiracy to commit criminal mischief, and criminal intent and fined $40 for failure to use a light on their raft. They were released on a PTA and the charges were eventually dropped.

KAIROS PLOWSHARES TOO: On August 1, 1988 Kathleen Maire and Anne Montgomery, continued their Kairos plowshares process by entering the EB facility in Quonset Point, RI, where they hammered and poured blood on Trident submarine parts. They held a banner which read: "Trident D-5 Into Plowshares" and were quickly apprehended. They were charged with malicious mischief and trespass and then released on a PTA. On September 27 they were tried by a judge in S. Kingston, RI. In a trial that lasted only 90 minutes, they were convicted by the judge of the above charges. They were sentenced to 6 months supervised probation and ordered to pay $250 in restitution for the fence they cut. After Kathy and Anne told the judge that, for reasons of conscience, they wouldn't pay the restitution or cooperate with probation, he changed their probation to "unsupervised" and fined them $250, which they refused to pay.

CREDO PLOWSHARES: On September 20, 1988 Marcia Timmel, of the Plowshares #4, mother and member of the Olive Branch Catholic Worker in Washington, D.C., entered the Sheraton-Washington hotel in D.C. - site of the Air Force Association Arms Bazaar. Once inside she hammered and poured blood on a Textron Defense System (TDS) MX missile display, thereby dismantling it, and was subsequently arrested. She left at the site a statement decrying the blasphemous theme of the Arms Bazaar, "Freedom: A Creed To Believe In," and issued her own creed (credo) of life, faith and love for the human family. During her two-day jury trial in D.C. Superior Court she used promotional literature of TDS, producer of the MX, to demonstrate the clear intent of TDS and the Air Force to prevail on Congress for the deployment of 50 new MX missiles. "We've been making $200 million a year for the last 10 years on this," said a TDS employee. "She took that model down the first day of the exhibition and we couldn't use it. She probably deprived us of a chance to persuade a couple members of Congress." Under the constraints of a jury instruction that relieved the government prosecution of the need to prove evil intent, the jury convicted Marcia on November 18, 1988 of property damage. On December 29, she was sentenced to 90 days; 83 days suspended pending completion of probation (90 days), and ordered to serve 7 days beginning January 9, 1989.

DUTCH DISARMAMENT ACTION: On December 8, 1988 the first anniversary of the INF Treaty, 12 Dutch peace activists, calling themselves "INF Ploughshares," cut through fences to enter the Woensdrecht Airbase and made their way to cruise missile bunkers where they carried out the first disarmament action in Holland. In their action statement they declared: "The INF Treaty was signed to eliminate the ground launched cruise and Pershing missiles from Europe. But the amount of air and sea launched missiles for European battlefield is increasing enormously and NATO plans are ready to modernize nuclear forces in Europe. The bunkers of cruise missiles won't be destroyed but given a new military destination. We oppose these new steps in the arms race We have started demolishing the Cruise missile bunkers by beating the bunker steel into ploughshares with sledgehammers. We demand that the money destined for new arms be spent instead on producing food for the hungry, detoxifying toxic waste dumps and cleaning polluted water." They were subsequently apprehended and most were released by Dutch authorities after being held for thirty hours. Kees Koning was released after eight days.

NF-5B PLOWSHARES: On January 1, 1989, Kees Koning, an ex-army chaplain and priest; and Co van Melle, a medical doctor working with homeless people and illegal refugees; both of whom participated in the INF disarmament action, entered the Woensdrecht Airbase once again, and began the conversion of NF-5B fighter airplanes by beating them with sledge hammers into ploughshares. The Dutch planned to sell the NF-5B to Turkey, for use against the Kurdish nationalists as part of a NATO-aid program which involves shipping of 60 fighter planes to Turkey. They were charged with trespass, sabotage and $350,000 damage. They were detained in jail through their trial and received nationwide media attention. They were tried before three judges on February 9, 1989. Among those who were allowed to testify at the trial were a Kurdish lawyer, a former Dutch air force officer, and Phil Berrigan. They were convicted and given the following sentences: Co Van Melle was sentenced to 7 months in prison, 3 months suspended and 2 years probation; and Kees Koning was sentenced to 8 months in prison, 2 months suspended and 2 years probation. They were released pending appeal. Their appeal was denied on November 17, 1989.

Other Dutch Disarmament Actions:

On February 9, 1989 Dutch activists Ad Hennen and Rolland van Hell, who were inspired by the two previous disarmament actions, entered a Dutch military base and started the conversion of Hawk missiles with axes. Ad was released pending trial but was detained because of his previous record. On April 5, 1989 they went to trial and were convicted. They were sentenced to 6 months in prison, plus a 4-month suspended sentence and 2 years probation. Ad was released pending their appeal. Their appeal was denied on November 17, 1989.

On Good Friday, March 24, 1989 Kees Konning, who had participated in the first two Dutch disarmament actions, entered a Dutch airbase and with a pick-axe began disarming a fighter plane destined for Turkey. He was subsequently arrested and imprisoned. On May 31, 1989 Kees went to trial. The state prosecutor demanded 18 months imprisonment but had failed to observe that Kees had disarmed the same plane he hammered on January 1, 1989. The judges ruled that he could not damage something he already damaged before and released him immediately.

On July 16, 1989 the anniversary of the first nuclear explosion named "Trinity," Kees Koning entered the Valkenburg Air Base in the Netherlands, and with a sledgehammer, began to disarm a P-3 Orion nuclear-capable airplane. Simultaneously, other Dutch activists entered the base and reclaimed the land by starting to cultivate it for life instead of death. Kees was arrested and imprisoned and began a fast which lasted until August 9, 1989. Following a trial he was convicted on September 12, 1989 and sentenced to 6 months in prison. On November 17th, following an appeal hearing for his January 1, 1989 action, Kees began a fast to demand an end to Dutch weapons sales to Turkey. He ended his fast on December 15, 1989. In the spring of 1990 Kees was released from prison.

STOP WEAPONS EXPORTS-PLOWSHARES 2: On February 16, 1989 the first Plowshares action occurred in Sweden. Anders Grip, a truck driver who works with a group providing material aid to the Third World, and Gunilla Akerberg, a consultant for organic farming, entered a railroad yard in Kristinehamn where weapons waited to be shipped to an Indian boat on the west coast of Sweden. They damaged the loading mechanism of the Haubits 77B mobile anti-aircraft missile launcher with hammers. This launcher was produced by the Bofors arms company. They then displayed a banner saying: "Disarmament has begun," "We must dare to be disobedient," "Violence and oppression depend upon our obedience and passivity." When the police came a half-hour later, Anders and Gunilla had set up a dining table and invited the police to join them in a meal. They were placed under arrest. On their way to the police station several of the police expressed support for their action and advised them of another potential site for a plowshares action. They were released later that night. They were sentenced to pay $10,000 in restitution to Bofors which they refused to pay. Bofors later dropped its request.

THAMES RIVER PLOWSHARES: Early in the morning on Labor Day, September 4, 1989 Jackie Allen, artist and shelter worker of the Ahimsa Community in Voluntown, CT and member of Griffiss Plowshares; Kathy Boylan, mother, sanctuary worker and member of the Long Island Catholic Peace Fellowship; Art Laffin, member of the Isaiah Peace Ministry and Trident Nein; and Elmer Maas, member of the Isaiah Peace Ministry and participant of two previous plowshares actions; Anne Montgomery, participant in five previous plowshares actions; Jim Reale, arborist and member of Jonah House; and Homer White, husband and member of the Caritas Community in Chapel Hill, NC; swam and canoed up the Thames River to the USS Pennsylvania Trident submarine, docked at the Naval Underwater Systems Center in New London, CN. Jackie, Anne, Kathy and Homer swam to the Trident. In full view of armed security, Jackie and Kathy hammered and poured blood on the Trident near the conning tower, while Anne was detained at the Trident dock. Jackie also carved the word "death" on the Trident. After 30 minutes Jackie and Kathy, who were fire-hosed by sailors, were taken into custody by the Coast Guard. Heavy tidal currents forced Homer to return to shore and he was arrested upon entering the main gate of the Naval Underwater Systems Center.

THE PLOWSHARES CHRONOLOGY 1980-2003
[43]

Simultaneously, Art, Elmer, and Jim canoed to the tail end of the Trident and, in full view of armed security, hammered and poured their blood on the side of the sub. They boarded the Trident, hammered several more times, and prayed, sang and read from St. John's Gospel for 45 minutes. They too were fire-hosed before taken into custody. They left on the Trident a videotape of live footage of Hiroshima after the bombing, a Salvadoran cross, a banner, booklets documenting the nuclear arms race at sea and naval nuclear accidents, their action statement and "Call to Confession and Captivity." Concurrently with this action, a 96 foot-long banner was dropped over the Gold Star Bridge in New London, proclaiming "Trident Is The Crime." After being held overnight in jail, they were arraigned and released the next day on a PTA. Charges were later dropped against Homer, presumably due to insufficient evidence. During their 3-day trial in Hartford Federal Court, they focused on their "lack of criminal intent" and on the criminality of the Trident, despite certain restrictions imposed by the court. Citing a ruling made by the Silo Pruning Hooks judge, their trial judge, Judge Nevas, instructed the jury to disregard the defendants' and their character witnesses' religious, moral and political views about the U.S. nuclear weapons policy. On December 19, they were convicted by a jury of conspiracy to enter a naval reservation for an unlawful purpose.

All, except Jackie, were acquitted of trespass with intent to injure and deprecate U.S. property. In addition, Jackie was the only one charged and convicted of destruction of government property less than $100. (During the trial the government entered into evidence one photo of hammer marks on the Trident, where Jackie said she hammered. Kathy claimed responsibility for some of the hammer marks in the photo. Despite each of the Thames River Plowshares conveying to the jury and the Court that they should all be treated the same way for their community act of disarmament, Jackie still was convicted of these charges. On March 6, 1990 they were given the following sentences: Jackie, Kathy, Art, Elmer, and Jim were sentenced to 60 days in prison; Anne was given a 120-day sentence. On January 7, 1991 the U.S. Court of Appeals for the Second District denied an appeal made by Jackie, Elmer, Jim and Art.

PLOWSHARES ESKILTUNA: On March 20, 1990 three Swedish peace activists, Lasse Gustavsson, Linus Brohult and Johan Hammarstedt, entered the FFV-Ordinance weapons factory in Eskilstuna, Sweden and disarmed the Carl-Gustaf bazooka with hammers. Their hammers were covered with pictures of their families. Seeking to stop the deadly export of Swedish weapons, the activists disarmed the Carl-Gustaf bazooka because it had been used in

Vietnam and was smuggled to Saudi Arabia via Great Britain during the 1980's. The U.S. also buys these bazookas. In a statement distributed to employees explaining the purpose of their action, the plowshares activists wrote: "By living the way we do we support war and injustice. Swedish weapons are used in warfare all over the world. It is the responsibility of each and every one of us to contribute to disarmament. By disarming Swedish weapons we hope to break through paralysis and powerlessness and instead help achieve peace and justice." On March 5, 1991 they were tried and convicted in Eskiltuna's District Court. They were ordered to pay $900 in restitution which they have refused to pay.

UPPER HEYFORD PLOWSHARES: Early on March 21, 1990, the first day of spring, British peace activists Stephen Hancock and Mike Hutchinson carried out the first British plowshares action. They entered the Upper Heyford U.S. Air Base and hammered on the outside of an F-111 fighter plane and then climbed into the cockpit where they also hammered on the nuclear weapons control panel. They left inside the plane a piece of the Berlin Wall and a statement that the INF treaty was a fraud because it eliminated no nuclear weapons. The F-111's, made by General Dynamics, are nuclear capable supersonic strike fighter planes which were used in the bombing raids against Libya in 1986. Their low level navigation and weapons delivery capability allows bombing at night and in adverse weather. Both activists wore "Mickey Mouse" ears, as they explained, "to have a friendly silhouette" for Americans guarding the base and its material. They also wore sheets that said: "Mickey Mouse Fan Club - Peace Section." They pinned on the side of the F-111 a banner that reiterated the message of their action and the statement "Isaiah was Here!" The two were arrested and held by the Ministry of Defense police and charged with "suspicion of criminal damage" amounting to 200,000 pounds. They were released on bail after serving 7 days in jail. On September 4, 1990 a jury found Mike and Steve guilty of damaging the aircraft and possessing mallets and fluid with intent to damage property. They were sentenced to 15 months imprisonment. They were released on parole on March 7th and were on probation through June 1991.

DOVES OF PEACE DISARMAMENT ACTION: On April 3, 1990 Susan Rodriguez, a longtime peace and community activist from Hayward, CA, entered the Physics International Laboratory on San Leandro, CA, a company which uses computers to simulate nuclear weapons explosions and research their effects on military hardware. She proceeded through several computer labs, and used a small sledgehammer to disarm several computers. When finally confronted by the police, she stopped and was arrested. Susan had learned of PI's relationship to the military industry in the course of her work for a computer repair company. On December 14, 1990 she was tried and convicted by a jury of two felony counts: burglary and malicious mischief (causing more than $25,000 worth of damage). On March 20, 1991 Susan was sentenced to one year in jail, suspended, 750 hours community service, three years probation and $1,000 restitution.

ANZUS PEACE FORCE PLOWSHARES: Early in the morning on January 1, 1991 Moana Cole, a Catholic Worker from New Zealand, Ciaron O'Reilly, a Catholic Worker from Australia, and Susan Frankel and Bill Streit, members of the Dorothy Day Catholic Worker in Washington, D.C., calling themselves the Anzus (Australia, New Zealand and U.S.) Peace Force Plowshares, entered the Griffiss Air Force Base in Rome, NY. After cutting through several fences, Bill and Sue entered a deadly force area and hammered and poured blood on a KC-135 (a refueling plane for B-52's) and then proceeded to hammer and pour blood on the engine of a nearby cruise missile armed B-52 bomber that could be used in the Middle East. They presented their action statement and an indictment to base security who encircled them moments later.

Simultaneously, Moana and Ciaron entered the base at the opposite end of the runway, and made a sign of the cross with blood on the runway, spray-painted "Love Your Enemies - Jesus Christ," "No More Bombing of Children in Hiroshima, Vietnam, Iraq, or Anywhere!" and "Isaiah Strikes Again." For approximately one hour they hammered upon the runway chipping at two sections, one being nearly 5 feet in diameter, before they were detained. In their action statement they declared that they came together from three different countries to reclaim the acronym from the ANZUS Treaty and create a "new pact for peace, which is the way of the Lord." They also asserted they were acting to prevent war in the Persian Gulf and called upon people to nonviolently resist war and oppression. In their indictment they cited the U.S. government for war crimes and violations of international law.

All four were indicted on January 9th on federal charges of conspiracy and property destruction and faced a maximum sentence of 15 years in prison. After being held in jail for over two months, they accepted pre-trial release on March 6th. They went to trial in Federal Court in Syracuse in May and were convicted by a jury. On August 20th, they were sentenced to twelve months in prison and ordered to pay $1800 in restitution. After serving 10 months Bill and Sue were released from prison in mid-June 1992. Moana and Ciaron were released in late June on bail pending a deportation hearing. In

October 1992, Moana returned to New Zealand following her court-ordered voluntary deportation. Ciaron returned to Australia on April 7th following his deportation hearing on March 29th.

ARMS FACTORY PLOWSHARES: On March 1, 1991 three Swedish peace activists: Stefan Falk, Anders Grip and Per Herngren, of the Pershing Plowshares, entered with the morning shift at the Swedish Ordnance's armaments factory in Ekilstuna, Sweden. Once inside, they disarmed with hammers two Carl Gustaf grenade throwers and one AK-5 automatic rifle. Their act of disarmament was met by workers, guards, and later the police, calmly and without violence. The three were placed under arrest, charged with unlawful entry and property damage, and later released. (Swedish Ordnance is a major producer of Swedish weapons and the largest share of its production is for export. The Carl Gustaf grenade thrower is distributed worldwide and was used extensively used in the Persian Gulf). They were tried and convicted in the spring of 1994. Per and Stephan were given fines while Anders was sentenced to 1 month in jail.

AEGIS PLOWSHARES: Before dawn on Easter, March 31st, 1991 Phil Berrigan, from Jonah House and participant in two previous plowshares actions; Kathy Boylan, member of the Thames River Plowshares and the Gulf Peace Team, from Long Island, NY; Tom Lewis, participant in the Transfiguration Plowshares East action from Worcester, MA; Barry Roth, psychiatrist and peace worker from Worcester, MA; and Daniel Sicken, an Air Force veteran and war-tax resister from Brattleboro, VT, boarded the USS Gettysburg, an Aegis-equipped Cruiser docked at the Bath Iron Works in Bath, ME. (According to the Navy, Aegis is "the most capable surface launched missile system the Navy has ever put to sea.") They proceeded to hammer and pour blood on covers for vertical launching systems for cruise missiles. They also left at the site their action statement which said in part, "We witness against the American enslavement to war at the Bath Iron Works, geographically near the President's home." They also left an indictment charging President Bush, Secretary of War Cheney, the National Security Council and the Joint Chiefs of Staff with war crimes and violations of God's law and international law, including the killing of thousands of Iraqis. They spent nearly two hours on the ship and in the yard before turning themselves into a member of the security force. After rejecting unsecured bond in court on April 1st, all five were released unconditionally on April 3rd pending trial by the state of Maine on charges of criminal trespass. Without explanation, the state decided against prosecuting them.

DARWIN PLOWSHARES: Early on August 17, 1991, Anthony Gwyther, of the West End Catholic Worker in Brisbane, Australia, entered Darwin RAAF base. He poured blood on a U.S. B-52 bomber, in Darwin to participate in the "Pitch Black '91" joint military exercises. He hammered on the bomb bay doors and inside the bomb bay area of the area of the aircraft beginning its conversion into implements to serve life. Anthony was then arrested by RAAF personnel to whom he gave his "Statement of Intent." He was held at Berrimah Police Headquarters for questioning and was released on bail. His hammer, bearing the inscription "Everyone beneath their vine and fig tree, unafraid (Micah 4:4)," his banner reading "Beat Swords Into Plowshares," and a copy of the video "Nowhere To Hide," made in Iraq during the height of U.S. bombing by Ramsey Clark, were taken from him to be used as evidence in court. Anthony was charged with "criminal trespass" and "criminal damage" under the Northern territory Criminal Code and with "trespass on Commonwealth property." He was tried and convicted in mid-December 1992 and was sentenced to three months in jail and ordered to pay a fine of $4369.

SOLDIER DISARMS RIFLE: On January 8, 1992, Magnus Eklund, a twenty-two year old Swedish conscript, disarmed his AK4 automatic rifle with a household hammer. Upon completing his action he told his officers he intended to refuse service and identified himself as a conscientious objector. He was held in the military barracks overnight before being reported to the civil police. In his statement he explained: "I want to put an end to my own violence and show my fellow soldiers that there are conscripted soldiers who don't accept militarism... I wish we could be a little less frightened to disobey. We have to trust our own thoughts. Big structures, like militarism, do, after all, depend on single individuals." He was sentenced to four months in prison.

GOOD FRIDAY PLOWSHARES MISSILE SILO WITNESS: On Good Friday morning, April 17, 1992, about 50 people accompanied Fr. Carl Kabat and Carol Carson as they caravanned to the Missile Silo Site #N5 at Whiteman AFB in Missouri, the same silo the Carl and other members of the Silo Pruning Hooks disarmed in 1984. They cut through a fence and once inside, Carol used a sledgehammer on the concrete lid of the silo while Carl performed a rite of exorcism. A half an hour later, two Air Force security guards arrived in a jeep. They ordered Carol and Carl to leave the silo compound and to face away from their supporters and the silo. But the crowd of supporters calmly proceeded to link arms and lovingly surround Carl and Carol. When the two security guards tried to separate them, small groups of people would return to the circle for song and prayer. Eventually the police arrived and Carol and Carl were arrested. Both were jailed and held until their court appearance on April 29th. At that time, Carol and Carl made a preliminary agreement with federal prosecutors whereby Carol and Carl would plead "no contest" to trespass in exchange for the property destruction charged being dropped. On May 15th, Carl and Carol were sentenced to six and three months in a halfway house.

HARRIET TUBMAN-SARAH CONNOR BRIGADE DISARMAMENT ACTION: Before dawn on May 10, 1992, Keith Kjoller, a peace activist, graphic artist and cinema worker from Santa Cruz, CA; and Peter Lumsdaine, a father, peace worker, writer from Santa Cruz, entered a secure area of the Space Systems complex at Rockwell International in Seal Beach, CA, wearing Rockwell shirts and work clothes. They entered Building 86 where they used wood-splitting axes to break open steel-mesh reinforced windows and a door of two dust-free "clean rooms" containing nine NAVSTAR global positioning satellites, which were being readied for delivery to the U.S. Air Force. Delicate components in the seven uncompleted satellites were also exposed to potentially damaging unfiltered air as well as tiny fragments of metal and glass. One completed NAVSTAR was struck 60 times with an ax. (This satellite, awaiting shipment to the NAVSTAR launch complex at Cape Canaveral, had to be completely disassembled by Rockwell technicians to assess and repair the damage, which totaled $2.75 million). As they were about to ax another satellite, Peter was seized at gunpoint while Keith was assaulted and choked unconscious by Rockwell personnel—despite both activists declaring themselves unarmed and intending not to threaten or struggle with them. They were then taken into police custody.

The NAVSTAR GPS system, is increasingly used for guiding advanced U.S. weapons and military/police assault teams to their targets—from bombers and cruise missiles during the Gulf War to counterinsurgency/search-and-destroy operations throughout the Third World. NAVSTAR is central to Pentagon preparations for launching a nuclear first-strike. Keith and Peter named their disarmament effort "The Harriet-Tubman Sarah Connor Brigade," honoring the historical conductor of the "underground railroad" and the fictional nuclear resistance fighter of the popular movie Terminator 2: Judgment Day. In their action they sought to commit maximum damage, thereby challenging plowshares and the wider disarmament movement to go beyond symbolic witness in addressing the war machines key technologies. Unlike other disarmament or plowshares actions, they also intended to flee Rockwell if they were able to following their action.

THE PLOWSHARES CHRONOLOGY 1980-2003

Held initially on $1 million bond and "preventive detention," their case was assigned to an FBI "investigation and terrorism" agent; and they were charged with damaging property manufactured for the U.S. government, a felony carrying up to ten years. Choosing to direct resources toward resistance organizing rather than a trial by an unjust government, they entered into a "guilty" plea agreement. Their bond was reduced to $50,000 and they were released in mid-June for four weeks under electronic monitoring. On September 21, 1992, in accordance with the "guilty" plea agreement, Peter was sentenced to two years prison, and Keith to eighteen months: with three years probation and $15,000 restitution being ordered for each of them by U.S. Judge Gary Taylor, who acknowledged the historical legacy of civil disobedience in his court room. Keith was released on parole from Lompoc Federal Prison in late September 1993 and Peter was transferred to a halfway house in December 1993 and in March 1994 was released on parole.

BAe PLOWSHARES: On January 6, 1993, feast of the Epiphany, Chris Cole, a Christian peace activist from Oxford, England, entered the British Aerospace (BAe) weapons factory in Stevenage, Herts, and used a household hammer to disarm a radar dome mold for the European Fighter Aircraft, a nose cone, a computer and the Hawk strike attack aircraft. He also poured blood on military equipment and carried two banners which said: "HEAL THE WORLD - HAMMER BAe SWORDS INTO PLOWSHARES" and "PREPARE THE WAY OF THE LORD - SWORDS INTO PLOWSHARES." The hammer and one of the banners were also used in the "Anzus Plowshares" action at Griffiss AFB in 1991. In a statement he left at the site he explained: "The Epiphany remembers when three men presented gifts to the infant Jesus. My gift of disarmament is for all the infants who are threatened with BAe weapons, from Northern Ireland to East Timor." (BAe is a heavy supplier of Hawk fighter planes to Indonesia. These planes, in turn, are used against the people of East Timor). After being at the site for about an hour, during which time he entered several buildings, he was arrested and jailed. On January 7th, he was charged with having caused criminal damage in excess of 475,000 pounds (about $700,000). He was released from prison on 10,000 pounds in June 1993 and given strict bail conditions pending trial.

On October 7, 1993, Chris was tried by a jury. Following eloquent testimony by Chris concerning BAe's criminal activity and how he had tried a variety of methods to appeal to BAe to disarm, the judge instructed the jury that they must use their "conscience, common sense and common humanity" to decide their verdict. The judge also told the jury that "if what Mr. Cole says is happening in East Timor, it may amount to genocide, which is a crime against

British and International law." On October 11th, the jury deliberated on the case for five hours and could not reach a verdict—at least three members of the jury thought Chris had done the right thing. Thus the trial ended in a hung jury. Four days later Chris had a new trial. This time he was convicted and sentenced to eight months imprisonment. He was released shortly after his conviction for he had already served the required time for this sentence.

GOOD NEWS PLOWSHARES: Before dawn on Good Friday, April 9, 1993, Kathy Boylan, participant in two previous plowshares actions, Greg Boertje-Obed, participant in three other plowshares actions and Michele Naar-Obed from Jonah House, entered the Newport News Shipbuilding in Newport News, VA wearing badges identifying themselves as "disarmers." After cutting through a fence they proceeded to the USS Tucson fast attack submarine. They scaled 80 feet of scaffolding, and climbed aboard. They then disarmed two Tomahawk cruise missile launchers by removing the inner metal casings and hammering on them with household hammers. They also poured blood onto these launchers as well as on a third Tomahawk launcher. The three spray painted "DISARM-CHRIST LIVES", "LOVE", and the sign of Christ's cross. They also displayed signs and hung banners. They left at the site a five-page indictment against the government for its war preparations and asserted that fast-attack submarines, which carry vertically launched, nuclear and conventional Tomahawk cruise missiles, are being illegally constructed at Newport News Shipbuilding. These missiles, carrying conventional warheads, were used during the U.S. massacre of Iraq and were responsible for much of the slaughter of Iraqi civilians and military.

After they completed their action, they prayed, sang and explained the purpose of their action to a nearby worker whom they had encountered during their action. The worker called security and they were taken into custody and placed under arrest. They were charged with state charges of "wanton trespass," a misdemeanor, and "destruction of property", a felony which carries a five year maximum sentence, and taken to the Newport News City Jail where they were held on $1500 bond. On May 4, 1993, they were tried by a judge on the trespass charge and given a $100 fine. Their trial was held in closed session because the judge cleared the court when supporters applauded as Greg, Michele and Kathy entered the courtroom. On August 24th they were tried by a jury (this time on the property destruction charge), convicted, sentenced and released—all in one day. Despite attempts by the prosecutor and the judge to limit their testimony, the three were given some latitude to speak and offered eloquent testimony.

However, in response to the judge trying to restrict Michele's closing statement, Greg explained to the court that they could no longer continue with the trial and invited supporters to join with them in singing "Rejoice In the Lord Always." Marshals removed the three from the courtroom, along with 15 supporters, who were taken to holding cells in the courthouse. When the jury reached a decision about the verdict and the sentencing, the three returned to the courtroom. They were found guilty and sentenced to eight months and a $2,500 fine (which they refuse to pay). Supporters earlier taken into custody were released. And after serving 4½ months in jail, Kathy, Greg and Michele were released for they had already served the required time for an eight-month sentence.

JAS INTO PLOWSHARES: On June 22, 1993 Swedish peace activists Pia Lundin and Igge Olsson entered a hanger at SAAB Military Aircraft factory in Linkoping, Sweden and proceeded to hammer on the bomb mountings underneath the wings of JAS (Hunting Attack Scanning), an attack reconnaissance plane. They sowed wheat on the factory grounds and awaited their arrest. When the police arrived to arrest them, they were offered cherries and invited to share bread and water with them, thereby symbolizing that the resources of the earth are enough for everyone when they are shared. Authorities alleged that there was $200,000 in damages. On July 16th they were tried and convicted of "malicious damage." On June 24th, peace activists Thomas Falk and Hans Leander entered the SAAB plant, intending to hammer on three of the four remaining JAS planes (the last plane would be left as a symbol of the need for more people to come forward to disarm it). Upon entering the factory they were apprehended, and thereby unable to carry out their part of the action. They were charged with aiding and attempt to "sabotage" and convicted of aiding and attempting to do "malicious damage."

In October 1993, the four were sentenced to 1 year in prison and ordered to pay $80,000 in restitution to SAAB. They were released from prison in August and November 1994. Not wanting to give money to arms production, the group offered SAAB a deal where the group would raise the $80,000 and give it to a water well project in India instead of to SAAB. SAAB responded positively from the beginning but when it became clear to them that the activists would not stop the resistance until the factory was converted, they ended the dialogue and handed their request over to the "Kronofogde" (corresponds to IRS in USA). The group decided to resist the Kronofogde and raise the money for the water well project.

PAX CHRISTI-SPIRIT OF LIFE PLOWSHARES: Early on the morning of December 7, 1993, Phil Berrigan, a participant in three previous plowshares actions; John Dear, a Jesuit priest, author, and peace activist who works with the homeless in Washington, D.C.; Lynn Fredriksson, a peace activist who works with the homeless in Baltimore, and Bruce Friedrich, a member of the Dorothy Day Catholic Worker in Washington, D.C., entered the Seymour Johnson AFB in Goldsboro, North Carolina. Coincidentally, the base was going through special war game exercises and maneuvers on this anniversary of Pearl Harbor. Wading through water and crossing rough terrain, the four made their way past hundreds of Air Force personnel and approached a nuclear capable F-15E fighter plane. (The F-15E, which costs $40 million, is capable of carrying both nuclear and conventional weapons, and was the mainstay of the U.S.-led attack on Iraq). They proceeded to hammer on bomb pylons, the main bomb guidance antenna, the cockpit undercarriage, one guidance light, and the Lantern all-weather flight pod.

Additionally, they removed the air intake covers and poured blood in the air intakes and over the side of the plane. They also placed on the ground their statement and an indictment charging the base and the U.S. government with crimes against peace and humanity along with their banner which read: "DISARM AND LIVE." After several minutes, they were surrounded by hundreds of Air Force soldiers, some screaming: "This is the real world." They were charged in Federal Court with destruction of government property, a felony. Stating that they could not comply with a court order not to return to the base they were held without bond. After being denied advisory counsel by their judge, and after having their trial date changed three times, the four appeared in Federal Court in Elizabeth City, NC on February 15th to begin their jury trial. Before the trial began, the prosecutor introduced an "Motion In Limine" which would prohibit the defendants from being able to speak about their moral and political justification for their action. When they were not allowed by the judge to finish their opening statement to the jury, they turned their backs to the judge as about twenty supporters joined them in saying Lord's Prayer and singing peace songs. Lynn, John and Bruce were held in contempt of court along with six supporters. (David Sawyer, an African-American supporter, was assaulted by U.S. marshals and was, in turn, charged with assault. He spent three weeks in jail and was released on bond—a plea agreement was later worker out).

Meanwhile, the other six supporters were given six-month sentences, however, five were released on March 9th and 10th and placed on 1 year supervised probation. Brad Sjostrom was imprisoned for three months and then placed on 1 year supervised probation. Judge Boyle later that afternoon declared a mistrial stating that the jury had been "contaminated." The four plowshares defendants were sent back to jail. Seeking to deter possible further courtroom resistance, Judge Boyle ordered that the four be given separate jury trials. He also ordered that each defendant have standby advisory counsel. With the judge threatening the defendants in advance with contempt of court should they defy any of his rulings, the prosecutor and the judge strongly enforcing the Motion In Limine "gag order" on the defendants and the U.S. Marshalls tightly restricting supporter's admission into the courtroom, defendants and supporters witnessed what were perhaps the most repressive plowshares trials to date. In each of the trials the four were repeatedly objected to by vindictive prosecutors and were constantly warned by the judge that the Bible, their religious views, the role of the F-15E fighter plane used to bomb Iraq and U.S. nuclear war preparations were irrelevant.

Phil was the only one of the four to take the stand to testify. And after Boyle's ruling that she could not give her opening statement to the jury because it was irrelevant, Lynn remained silent throughout her trial. Despite the court's attempt to suppress the truth, each of the four were able to powerfully and creatively witness to the truth of their action. Each were found guilty with the juries taking 1 hour for Phil, 30 minutes for John, 20 minutes for Lynn and 6 minutes for Bruce to return their verdicts. On July 6, 1994, the four were sentenced to the following: Phil--8 months in jail, 4 months house confinement, which he non-cooperated with; John--7½ months in jail, 4½ months house confinement; Lynn--14 months in jail; Bruce--15 months in jail. Each were given credit for time already served. They were also sentenced to 3 years of supervised probation and ordered to pay $2700 in restitution. In January of 1997 Bruce was sentenced to 5 months in jail and three months house arrest for a probation violation.

ANARCHIST PLOWSHARES: On January 27, 1994 activists Calle Hoglund and Karna Rusek entered the Satenas F7 base in Sweden as military exercises were being conducted. They proceeded to hammer on the nose cone of a Viggen-type military aircraft. The two were subsequently held in custody for five weeks. They were both charged and convicted of sabotage, a felony offense. Calle was sentenced to 14 months in prison and Karna to 3 months. On appeal Calle's sentence was reduced to 12 months. Ulf Lundblad, Mats Kolmisopi and Henrik Hoglund were also charged with aiding in this act of sabotage. Ulf and Henrik were sentenced to 8 months in prison and Mats, because he was under 18, was not given a prison sentence. Ulf and Calle began serving their sentence on November 27, 1995.

GOOD FRIDAY- APRIL FOOLS DAY PLOWSHARES: At noon on April 1, 1994 (Good Friday and April Fool's Day), Fr. Carl Kabat, still on parole for the Silo Pruning Hooks action, entered the Grand Forks Missile Field in North Dakota dressed as a clown. After cutting through a fence surrounding a Minuteman III missile silo (not scheduled to be deactivated under the START I agreement), he proceeded to hammer on a combination dial for the silo as well as the silo lid. He prayed, sang and hung a banner on the silo fence that said "Stop Nuclear Weapons." After about half an hour, a helicopter, a tank and 10 soldiers armed with machines guns arrived at the site and held him at the site for two hours. Meanwhile, Sam Day and Michael Sprong, who were outside the missile silo fence supporting Carl, were asked to leave. When they refused to do so they, too, were taken into custody and charged with trespass (this charge was later dropped). Carl was taken to the Barnes County Jail in Valley City, North Dakota. At a hearing the following Monday he was charged in State Court with trespass and malicious destruction of property—both felony charges—and was ordered held without bond. During his arraignment on April 13, Carl pled "no contest" to the charges against him and stated that his action was on behalf of the children of the world. On May 16th, Carl was sentenced to 5 years in prison and ordered to pay a $7,000 fine.

Following his release from prison, Carl was placed on probation for five years. On August 6, 2000, Carl, wearing a clown suit, offered a peace witness at a Minuteman III nuclear missile silo in northeast Colorado (site of the Minuteman III plowshares action), in violation of his probation. He was charged with trespass and released pending trial. On May 3, 2001 he was convicted by a jury in Federal

Court in Denver, Colorado. After 83 days in jail awaiting sentencing, he was sentenced to time served. Still facing five years probation from his plowshares action, Carl did not appear for an August 6 parole revocation hearing. He was arrested on August 14 as he attended the funeral of a fellow Oblate's mother at the Shrine of the Oblates of Mary Immaculate in Belleville, Illinois. He was sentenced to one year and a day. He was released from prison in early June 2002.

JUBILEE PLOWSHARES: On August 7, 1995 six religious peace activists carried out coordinated plowshares actions to commemorate the 50th anniversary of the U.S. atomic bombings of Hiroshima and Nagasaki. The following is an excerpt of their statement: "The period of August 6 through 9 marks the 50th anniversary of the nuclear destruction of Hiroshima and Nagasaki, Japan...Since August 1945 the entire world, led by the U.S. has been held hostage by nuclearism and the exponential rise of military violence. This violence permeates every level of society... Disarmament is the necessary first step to Christ's Jubilee. We refuse to see violence as inevitable, injustice as the order of the day, and death dealing as the only way of life. Join us in this declaration for disarmament to announce the jubilee for the poor, relief for the children, and peace for us all."

JUBILEE PLOWSHARES EAST: Before dawn, Michele Naar-Obed of the Good News Plowshares, Philadelphia activists Rick and Erin Sieber (father and son), and Amy Moose, a social worker and peace activist from New York City, entered Newport News Shipbuilding. They cut through a fence and walked to the USS Greenville fast attack submarine.

They boarded the submarine and proceeded to hammer and pour blood on the soft metal casing inside four vertical launch tubes for the Tomahawk cruise missile. They also pasted pictures of the Hiroshima victims to the submarine and laid out their statement and indictment. After a period of prayer they then spoke with a shipyard worker about their action, who in turn called security. The four were arrested and jailed at Newport News City jail and held on $6,500 bond. (Rick was released on bond several weeks later). The four were charged by the State of Virginia with trespass and destruction of property—a felony. On September 19th the four were tried on the trespass charge. Despite attempts by the court to suppress the truth, especially during cross-examination of Newport News personnel, the four were able to offer powerful testimony about their witness. They were convicted and immediately given the maximum sentence for this charge: 1 year in jail and a $2500 fine.

The four decided to appeal and be tried again on the trespass charge during their jury trial on the property destruction charge. Erin, Michele and Amy were released on bond several weeks later. Following their release Amy accepted a plea-bargain agreement due to personal reasons. Shortly before their expected jury trial in December, they were notified that state charges were being dropped and that they would be indicted on federal charges. On January 19th Erin, Rick and Michele pled not guilty to the following charges: damage to national defense material, conspiracy to damage national defense material, destruction of government property (submarine and shipyard fence), and conspiracy to commit destruction of government property. These charges carry a maximum sentence of 45 years in prison and a $12 million fine.

In April 1996 the group returned to court for a motions hearing. During this hearing international law expert, Matthew Lippman, testified about why nuclear weapons are in violation of International law and about the legal justification for nonviolent protest. His testimony was deemed inadmissible by Judge Rebecca Smith. Also numerous motions argued by Attorney Sebastian Graber to drop the sabotage charge were not granted. In light of the repressive nature of the court and the near certainty of a minimum 10-

THE PLOWSHARES CHRONOLOGY 1980-2003

year and a maximum 45-year prison sentence, the three decided to accept a plea agreement. Erin was sentenced to eight months (4 months in prison and four months house arrest on an electronic monitor) Rick was sentenced to 9 months imprisonment, and Michele was sentenced to 18 months imprisonment. They were each ordered to pay $6,000 in restitution. And they were all given three years of supervised probation.

Prior to her release, an anonymous donor paid Michele's restitution. Upon her release from prison, Michele was ordered by the Federal Probation Office in Baltimore not to return to Jonah House, her home community. Violating this order would mean Michele's having to spend substantially more time in prison. Based on past encounters with Jonah House, the FPO deemed that Jonah House was an unfit site for her rehabilitation. As a result of this denial of her right to return home, Michele, her husband and her daughter relocated to Norfolk, VA and then to the Catholic Worker in Duluth, MN. In the spring of 1999, Michele and her family returned to Jonah House whereupon she was cited with a probation violation. Judge Smith gave her a one-year prison sentence. She was released on June 21, 2000, finally free of probation and other restrictions that led to her exile.

JUBILEE PLOWSHARES WEST: Shortly after 8:00 a.m. Ukiah school-teacher and peace activist Susan Crane, and Steve Kelly, a Jesuit priest from Oakland, walked onto Lockheed-Martin Corporation in Sunnyvale, CA, builder of the first strike Trident II D-5 missile. They approached a large assembly building, and to their amazement, a large rolling door opened up. They walked into the building and proceeded to hammer and pour blood on missile casings. On a nearby desk, they found classified plans for the missile and poured blood on them. While Susan and Steve awaited their arrest they spoke with some of the workers and displayed photos of nuclear victims. They were both taken into custody by state authorities and then released after 48 hours. Federal authorities then ordered them back to court on August 11. They pled not guilty to felony charges of destruction of government property and conspiracy. Bond was set at $75,000 for Susan and $50,000 for Steve, which they refused.

On November 28 they were tried by a jury in San Jose Federal Court. During her testimony, Susan attempted to introduce the Nuremberg Principles into evidence. When she was stopped for the third time, supporters in the courtroom successively stood up and read from the Principles and read from the Bible. Federal marshals proceeded to remove 8 supporters from the building. Susan was also removed from the courtroom. When Steve refused to proceed with the trial the jury was removed. Eventually resuming her testimony, Susan challenged the judge, "I do not accept your authority...I do not know why I am not allowed to speak the highest law of the land." Steve also offered compelling testimony and both offered character witnesses. During cross-examination both refused to answer questions about who drove them to the site. Each received civil contempt charges. They were both found guilty and faced a maximum sentence of 15 years imprisonment. During their sentencing they explained to the court they would not comply with any form of supervised release. On March 13, 1996, both were sentenced to 10 months in prison (with credit for time served) and 100 dollars in court costs. Following their release from prison they both went underground until their participation in the Prince Of Peace Plowshares.

SEEDS OF HOPE - EAST TIMOR PLOUGHSHARES: On January 29, 1996, borough counselor Joanna Wilson from Merseyside, gardener Lotta Kronlid from Sweden, and nurse Andrea Needham from Kirby, carried out the third British Plowshares action. In the early morning they entered the British Aerospace military site at Warton, Lancashire and proceeded to disarm a Hawk warplane. They hammered on the radar nose of the plane and on the control panel. When they were finished with their work they were able to make some phone calls from inside the South Hanger to tell their friends and the press about their witness. They were then arrested by the police. The Hawk ground-attack airplane that they disarmed (jet number ZH 955) was part of an order destined to Indonesia. Indonesia has since 1975 (when East Timor declared its independence) been waging a genocidal war against the people of East Timor. More than 200,000 people have been killed, which is about one third of the pre-invasion population. The group stated that there is substantial evidence that Hawks from previous deals have been used by the Indonesian military to bomb civilians.

The arms export to Indonesia, and especially the Hawk deal, has been opposed by many people and groups all over Britain, the group says. But the government and BAe have refused to stop the sale. "These planes will soon be killing people in East Timor unless action is taken immediately to stop them", the group says. Another member of the group, Angie Zelter, an environmental campaigner from Norfolk, publicly stated she intends to carry out a future ploughshares action at BAe to continue the process of disarmament there.

The four women where held in remand until the trial in July, charged with illegal entry and criminal damage. During the seven-day trial, the women—three of whom defended themselves—said they were disarming the Hawk, not vandalizing it, claiming the action was justified because the plane was going to be used against the civilians of East Timor. (The Hawk was one of 24 sold by British Aerospace to the Indonesian dictatorship; similar planes previously shipped to Indonesia have been seen bombing and flying over East Timor—and dropping bombs there.)

Surprisingly the four were acquitted! The jury of seven men and five women took just over five hours to reach their not-guilty verdict, which Wilson called a "victory for justice" and a "victory for the people of East Timor." Zelter added, "We think we have a very good case to prove that British Aerospace is aiding and abetting murder."

The three women were imprisoned and charged with illegal entry and criminal damage. Another member of the group, Angie

THE PLOWSHARES CHRONOLOGY 1980-2003

Zelter, an environmental campaigner from Norfolk, England, who signed the action statement and vowed to do another ploughshares action at BAe, was arrested on February 7, 1997 as she was on her way to a public meeting to speak. She was jailed and reunited with the other three.

After six months of imprisonment and nine pre-trial court appearances, the jury trial for the four began on July 23, 1997 at the Liverpool Crown Court. Throughout the week, supporters organized teach-ins and vigils. The prosecution case took two days. It included numerous witnesses testifying from BAe, the prosecutor showing the jury the report the women left in the plane's cockpit, and allowing the jury to view the video they left on the pilot's seat which explains their motives. The defense case took three days. Each of the women testified, stating that they had a lawful excuse to disarm the Hawk because they were using reasonable force to prevent a greater crime. They also cited British legislation and International law that outlaws genocide. The report they left inside the plane, along with the video, proved very helpful as references in their defense. The high point of the trial was the testimony of Jose Ramos Horta, the leader of the East Timorese government in exile. Other witnesses who testified included John Pilger, the journalist who made the powerful film about the genocide in East Timor titled, "Death of a Nation." After several hours the jury rendered a "not guilty" verdict, the first of its kind for a plowshares action. BAe immediately issued an injunction against the women, prohibiting them from BAe facilities so as to prevent "further interference in its businesses." On August 1, 1997, the four women held a press conference calling for the prosecution of BAe for aiding and abetting murder in East Timor.

WEEP FOR CHILDREN PLOWSHARES: Early in the morning, on July 27, 1996, the day of the launching of the 18th Trident submarine, Sr. Elizabeth Walters, I.H.M., from Michigan; Sr. Carol Gilbert, O.P. and Sr. Ardeth Platte, O.P. from Jonah House; and Kathy Boylan from Dorothy Day Catholic Worker in Washington, DC, entered the Naval Submarine Base in Groton, CT. During their liturgy of disarmament they poured blood on a torpedo test cylinder used inside fast attack submarines. They then began a universal peace dance and sang, "We begin in the name of our God." They proceeded to hammer 18 times on the test cylinder, symbolic of their rejection of 18 Trident submarines that have been built. Once sailors and security appeared nearby, they put down their hammers decorated with rainbow ribbons and pictures of children, baby bottles with recorded messages of peace, and documents substantiating the immorality and illegality of nuclear weapons. They covered the weapon piece with a banner –*WEEP FOR CHILDREN PLOWSHARES* and knelt down and continued their liturgy. They were arrested by military and security personnel and charged with trespass and willful injury to government property. They were tried in U.S. Federal Court in Hartford in September. During closing remarks, the Prosecutor declared: "These women must be stopped because they are just like the Oklahoma City bomber!" Obviously amazed, Judge Thomas Smith firmly disagreed and stated that the women were following a higher law. They were sentenced to 1000 hours of community service.

PRINCE OF PEACE PLOWSHARES: In the pre-dawn hours on Ash Wednesday, February 12, 1997, Susan Crane and Steve Kelly, S.J, of the Jubilee Plowshares West; Steve Baggarly, husband and father from the Norfolk Catholic Worker; Mark Colville, father of three from the New Haven Catholic Worker; Tom Lewis-Borbely of the Transfiguration Plowshares East; and Phil Berrigan, member of several plowshares actions, boarded the USS The Sullivans, a nuclear-capable Aegis destroyer at Bath Iron Works in Maine. They hammered and poured blood on different parts of the battleship, including the pilot house, the bridge, the helicopter pad, and several missile hatch covers. As they read their action statement and unfurled a banner, armed military security forcibly pushed them to the deck and placed them under arrest.

During their jury trial in U.S. District Court in Portland, ME, they were not allowed to present expert witnesses, except for Daniel

THE PLOWSHARES CHRONOLOGY 1980-2003

Berrigan, S.J. whose testimony was restricted. Also U.S. marshals were ordered by the judge to limit access to the courtroom to supporters. The defendants were prevented by the judge from offering an international law defense based on the 1996 world court decision which deemed the possession of first strike nuclear weapons illegal. Most supporters were removed from the courtroom for singing and speaking out. On May 7 they were convicted of destruction of government property and conspiracy. They were each sentenced separately—three on Oct. 27 and three on Oct. 29. They were sentenced to the following prison terms: Susan, 27 months; Phil, 24 months; Steve Kelly, 21 months; Mark, 13 months; Steve Baggarly, 13 months; and Tom, 6 months. Each was given two years supervised probation and ordered to pay $4,703.89 in restitution. They were given credit for the time they had already served. Sentences were based on their past records as well as their cooperation during the trial. On both sentencing days people were arrested for nonviolent actions at BIW—10 of whom accompanied Susan for a night in jail.

Upon release from prison, Tom was ordered to pay restitution, which he refused to do. He was eventually given another four months in jail. Facing more substantial time in prison for failure to comply with restitution, an anonymous supporter paid Steve Baggarly's restitution following his release from prison. Susan was ordered not to return to Jonah House upon her release because it is a place of "ongoing criminal activity." After a period of time, she returned with the court's consent to Jonah House. She refused to pay restitution. Upon his release, Phil was ordered by the court not to associate with other convicted felons, except for his wife. He also refused to pay restitution. Mark refused to pay any restitution and the court informed him in May 2000 that it would serve no purpose to incarcerate him because his views still would not be changed. Steve Kelly refused payment of restitution. (Please see Plowshares VS. Depleted Uranium for an update on their further imprisonment.)

CHOOSE LIFE DISARMAMENT ACTION: On April 19, 1997, two Swedish peace activists, Cecelia Redner, a priest in the Church of Sweden, and Marija Fischer, a student, entered the Bufors Arms factory in Karlskoga, Sweden, planted an apple tree and attempted to disarm a naval canon being exported to Indonesia. Cecelia was charged with attempt to commit malicious damage and Marija with assisting. Both were also charged with violating a law which protects facilities "important to society."

Both women were convicted on February 25, 1998. They argued, over repeated interruptions by the judge, that, in Redner's words, "When my country is arming a dictator I am not allowed to be passive and obedient, since it would make me guilty to the crime of genocide in East Timor. I know what is going on and I cannot only blame the Indonesian dictatorship or my own government. Our plowshares action was a way for us to take responsibility and act in solidarity with the people of East Timor." Fischer added, "We tried to prevent a crime, and that is an obligation according to our law." Redner was sentenced to fines and three years of correctional education. Fischer was sentenced to fines and two years suspended sentence.

Both the prosecutor and defendants appealed the case. No jail sentence was imposed.

LAURENTIAN SHIELD TRIDENT ELF DISARMAMENT ACTION: On April 22, 1997, Earth Day, Donna and Tom Howard-Hastings used handsaws to cut down three poles supporting the ELF transmitter for the Trident submarine in northern Wisconsin. After the poles were cut they were decorated with photos of children and posted with documents about international law and treaties outlawing nuclear weapons. They also placed stakes to mark tree seedlings under the transmission lines that they say are "doomed to the cutting bar." They cut a section of one of the downed poles, carrying it to the nearby transmitter site where they turned themselves in to security personnel. They were then taken into custody by county sheriffs. An ABC TV news affiliate, along with reporters from two public radio stations were on hand to observe what happened. They were charged with sabotage and property destruction.

During their three-day jury trial in Ashland County District Court, they were allowed to present several expert witnesses, including retired Navy Captain Bush, Bob Aldridge and International law expert, Francis Boyle. They were acquitted of the sabotage charge, which carried ten years and $10,000 fine, but they were convicted of destruction of property. At their sentencing on December 3, they stated to the judge that the court had no jurisdiction over them, seeing that a jury had determined that their action was reasonable and that they did not damage the national defense. They also made a passionate appeal to the judge to heed International laws and the World Court decision to outlaw nuclear weapons. Donna was sentenced to 114 days she had already served, with a three-year period of probation and restitution. Tom was sentenced to 1 year in prison, with credit for time served and three years of intensive probation, including electronic home monitoring, and restitution.

The name Laurentian Shield refers to the name of the granite rock geological formation at the ELF site.

GODS OF METAL PLOWSHARES: On May 17, 1998, the 30th anniversary of the Catonsville Nine action, Sr. Carol Gilbert, OP, and Sr. Ardeth Platte. OP., previous plowshares participants from Jonah House; Fr. Larry Morlan of the Silo Plowshares; Fr. Frank Cordaro, from Des Moines, Iowa; and Kathy Boylan, past plowshares participant, disarmed a nuclear-capable B-52 bomber during the Department of Defense Open House at Andrews Air Force Base. As hundreds of spectators looked on, the five poured blood and hammered on the inside and outside of the bomb bay missile hatches and doors of the plane. Ardeth was temporarily restrained by a spectator but was able to rejoin the others. As the group began their action, Fr. Cordaro shouted: "Sisters and Brothers, let us disarm these gods of metal." The group then unfurled their banner, prayed and read their leaflet to those nearby which explained to onlookers the meaning of their action. They were then placed under arrest by base security. They were charged with depredation of government property and released.

On September 22, they were tried by a judge in U.S. Federal Court in Greenbelt, MD. Their two-day trial included moving testimony from each defendant, and International law expert, Francis Boyle, was allowed to testify. Following their conviction they requested immediate sentencing. When they were denied this request, they informed the court they could not promise to return for sentencing. They remained in jail until January 4, their sentencing date. Frank, Carol and Ardeth were sentenced to six months in jail while Larry was sentenced to four months imprisonment. Due to her previous record,

THE PLOWSHARES CHRONOLOGY 1980-2003

[65]

Kathy was given a 10-month prison sentence.

MINUTEMAN III PLOWSHARES: On August 6, 1998 at 6:00 AM, Daniel Sicken, an Air Force veteran and peace activist from Brattleboro, VT, and Sachio Ko-Yin, a nursery school teacher and activist from Ridgewood, NJ, entered silo N7 in Weld County near Greeley, Colorado operated by Warren AFB, Cheyenne, Wyoming. With sledgehammers they broke bolts on the tracks for opening the Minuteman III missile silo lid. In addition they poured blood on the silo, displayed a banner, and stenciled the picture of a broken rifle, the universal symbol of disarmament, along with the image of a

gravestone on the launching pad. They timed their action to coincide with the 53rd anniversary of the dropping of the first atomic bomb on Hiroshima. Addressing the fact that 500 Minuteman III missiles are still deployed, with each missile equivalent to the destructive power of 60 Hiroshima bombs, they declared: "In the spirit of nonviolence...we symbolically disarm and convert this site to a life-sustaining place. We give witness to our opposition to U.S. violations of the rights of this and future generations." They were arrested by armed security and jailed pending their trial.

In early November they were tried by a jury in U.S. District Court in Denver. They were not allowed to present an international law or justification defense. They were convicted by a jury of conspiracy, destruction of government property, and sabotage. Following their conviction, they were immediately imprisoned when they told the judge that, due to the court's upholding of the legitimacy of nuclear weapons, they could not return for sentencing.

U.S. District Judge Walker Miller faced the prospect of sentencing the defendants to 5-8 years imprisonment in January, the terms recommended by federal sentencing guidelines. "They didn't put a bomb in a bomber," he said. Miller postponed sentencing to consider written arguments for and against a shorter sentence. On February 18th, Dan was sentenced to 41 months, and Sachio to 30 months imprisonment. Both men were also ordered to pay $21,299.40 in restitution and perform 30 hours of community service per month for three years of supervised release. An Appeals Court denied a prosecution request to give Dan and Sachio additional prison time.

JABILUKA PLOWSHARES: In the early hours of August 9, 1998, the 53rd anniversary of the U.S. atomic bombing of Nagasaki, Ciaron O'Reilly, an Australian Catholic Worker and member of the Anzuz Plowshares, and Treena Lenthall, an advocate for people with disabilities and activist for a free East Timor from Australia, used house-hold hammers and bolt-cutters to disable uranium equipment at the Jabiluka uranium mine in Australia's Northern territory. Using baby bottles decorated with pictures of dying children from Nagasaki and Chernobyl, they poured blood onto excavation equipment. They wrote the names of nuclear radiation victims on the equipment—from Nagasaki to Three Mile Island to Iraq—exposing the lethal consequences caused by uranium. They then unfurled a banner: "Nuclear War and Poison Begin Here! Let's End It Here! Swords Into

THE PLOWSHARES CHRONOLOGY 1980-2003

Ploughshares." In their action statement they declared: "The nuclear weapons assembly line begins here at the Jabiluka uranium mine. Today we end it here with this nonviolent act of disarmament—the prophecy of Isaiah. The road from Jabiluka leads to Nagasaki, Hiroshima, Chernobyl, Muroroa, Missan...With this act of disarmament we begin to prepare the way of the Lord—a path of nonviolent resistance towards justice and peace." After one hour they were arrested by police, and held 5-7 weeks in Darwin Prison.

During a four day court case, they were permitted to testify about experiences and knowledge that compelled them to act. Treena was able to present to the court a video about Jabiluka. She was then acquitted of the fence-cutting charge. At a subsequent hearing on December 14, the Magistrate convicted her of trespass and one count of damage to the excavator. Ciaron was convicted of trespass and two counts of damage. They were sentenced to time served and ordered to pay $6673 restitution. Instead of paying restitution the two returned to the Jabiluka mine for a nonviolent witness on January 17, 2000. They were arrested and ordered to serve 66 days in prison.

HMS VENGEANCE DISARMAMENT ACTION: On November 23, 1999, Sylvia Boyes and River, British activists involved with the Trident Ploughshares 2000 campaign, swam with hand tools with the intent to disarm the HMS Vengeance Trident submarine at the Barrow Shipyard in England. They were apprehended by security before being able to reach the Trident and charged with conspiracy to commit criminal damage. Following their arrest they were released pending trial. During their six day jury trial in mid-January 2001, held at the Manchester Crown Court, the two argued that the intent of their action was to rid Britain of the illegal nuclear threat posed by Trident submarines. Expert witnesses testified about how direct action against nuclear weapons policy can be effective (i.e. bringing about the withdrawal of U.S. cruise missiles from England), and that Trident is not simply a defensive weapon, but has been deployed as a threat in recent conflicts. On January 18, the jury returned a majority verdict of not guilty.

ALDERMASTON WOMEN TRASH TRIDENT: Early on February 1, 1999, Rosie James and Rachel Wenham, both from Leeds, England and peace activists from the Aldermaston Women's Group, safely and nonviolently prevented a British Trident from temporarily leaving its dock as part of the Trident Ploughshares 2000 disarmament campaign. The two swam 300 meters in wet suits to the Barrow-in-Furness shipyard where the HMS Vengence Trident was docked. They swam in freezing conditions in the dark with their disarmament equipment of hammers, chisels, crowbars, screw-drivers and paint.

Once aboard the sub, they hung a banner on the conning tower, which read "Women Want Peace" and painted the words "Illegal Death Machine" and peace and women's symbols on the sub. The women then dismantled radio equipment used to launch weapons of mass destruction. The women were arrested and taken into custody. Three other supporters were later arrested as they brought dry clothes to Rachel and Rosie--their charges were soon dropped. Rosie was released the next afternoon and Rachel on Feb. 8. They were charged with criminal damage set at a cost of 25,000 pounds and were banned from Barrow.

During their trial in Manchester Crown Court, Justice Humphries ruled the defenses available within the Criminal Damage Act of necessity/duress and acting to protect property or life, could be left for the jury to decide on. The third legal defense offered—that of preventing a greater crime (in this instance the crime of genocide and the transgressions of various international laws of war)- could not be submitted to the jury. On September 20, the jury found Rosie and Rachel not guilty of one charge, and on the second charge the jury could not reach a verdict.

On October 4, 2001, another jury failed to convict the two and thus Crown prosecutors announced they would no longer pursue the case.

BREAD NOT BOMBS PLOUGHSHARES: On September 13, 1998, three Swedish peace activists, Annika Splade, a nurse and student of International Relations; Stellan Vinthagen, a Peace Researcher, and Ann-Britt Sternfeldt, an ex-town councillor, writer and administrator, were arrested within the perimeter fence of VSEL Barrow in England on suspicion of going equipped to commit criminal damage. One of the three had already begun to dismantle equipment outside of the "Devonshire Hall," the shed in which the HMS Vengeance, the fourth and final British Trident submarine is being constructed. They each acted in support of the Trident Ploughshares 2000 Campaign, a nonviolent direct action campaign to stop the Trident program.

Calling themselves "Bread Not Bombs Ploughshares", the three carried with them household hammers, and individual and group statements to the site. They also brought loaves of bread to symbolize the urgent need to feed the poor and to invest in life, not in weapons of death. In their statement they declared: "We are taking this action, as privileged people living in the First World, because nuclear weapons are a threat against all human beings and against future generations. As long as nuclear weapons exist, humanity is doomed to live in fear that they may be used." The three were arrested and jailed, and released on January 21, pending their trial. On March 18, they broke one of the few conditions of their release by

deliberately failing to make a fortnightly report to the Liverpool police. On March 21, they broke another condition of their release by returning to the Barrow shipyard with 20 supporters to ask workers and security to continue the disarmament work of the Trident. They were taken back into custody pending their trial.

After an eight-day trial, which was held in Preston, the judge instructed the jury that most of the evidence presented about international law was not admissible. However, it still made a great impact on the jury. The case resulted in a hung jury and the three were released.

On October 11, 1999, the government decided to retry the case. Ann-Britt was ill and unable to attend the new trial. With over 70 peace activists on hand from many countries, Annika and Stellan went through their second jury trial, which lasted five days. This time they were convicted, even though the verdict was not initially unanimous. They were sentenced to time already served. No further legal action has been taken to date against Ann-Brit.

TRIDENT THREE DISARMAMENT ACTION: On the evening of June 8, 1999, three Trident Ploughshares 2000 activists, Ellen Moxley, a retired zoologist and peace campaigner from Scotland; Ulla Roder, a shop assistant from Denmark and Angie Zelter, a potter and activist from Norfolk, England, disarmed a vital part of the Britain's Trident nuclear weapons system when they disabled "Maytime," a floating laboratory barge in Loch Goil, Scotland, which is used to check on the ability of individual submarines to avoid sonar detection. The Floating

Lab Complex is run by the Defense Evaluation and Research Agency (DERA), a prime supplier of technical advise to the U.K. Ministry of Defense.

Using an inflatable boat they made their way from shore to the Maytime. Once aboard, they unbolted a loose window and cut their way into the lab with chisels and wrecking bars and damaged 20 computers and other electronic equipment and circuit boxes, cut an antenna, jammed machinery with superglue, sand, and syrup and tipped logbooks, files, computer hardware, and papers overboard. They draped banners over the lab, reading "Stop Nuclear Death Research," and "TP2000 Opposes Research for Genocide." They then had a picnic of sandwiches and grapes. They were on board for four hours before MOD police, apparently alerted by a media inquiry, took them into custody. They were charged with malicious damage and theft. Authorities estimated the value of damage worth 80,000 pounds.

In their collective statement the women said: "Our actions are based on the legal and ethical premise that the U.K.'s Trident nuclear weapons system is a system preparing for the mass murder of innocent civilians over untold generations. As loving, feeling human beings, we feel responsible for trying to do everything in our power to prevent the system from being able to operate, providing that our actions are safe, nonviolent, open and accountable."

They were jailed for nearly four months before facing trial in October. Their trial in Edinburgh, Scotland, resulted in an acquittal. Of her acquittal Ellen stated: "For me what we did... was the culmination of a whole life-time of campaigning. I felt as if I was doing something worthwhile and acting for the 80 percent of people who don't want Trident in this country."

Although their acquittal could not be reversed the Scottish High Court of Justiciary issued a judgment on March 30, 2001 in response to the Lord Advocate's Reference to the acquittal of the Trident Three. The intent of this judgment was to set a precedent for future Trident resistance trials in Scottish courts. The ruling came at the time a poll showing that 51% of the Scottish people favored an upcoming Trident protest while 24% opposed the protest. In a 76 page text, a panel of three judges failed to challenge the illegality of Trident by answering in the negative four questions set by the Lord Advocate, thereby dismissing the claims of the three defendants. The chair of the panel gave a summary of the judgment in a few curt sentences and then hurried out of the courtroom. Trident resisters expressed great disappointment with the ruling and exposed the incompetent legal arguments of the judgment. A clear example of the lack of reasoning in the judgment is the claim that the question of Trident's legality can only be considered in a time of war. Trident resisters declared that common sense demands that if we are concerned at all about the legality of our weapons we examine the question as we prepare to deploy them--not wait until it is too late. The judgment completely ignored admissions made by the defendants regarding the applicability of the Geneva Convention and the Nuremberg Principles to Trident. Thus the High Court failed to answer the basic question: how could a 100 kiloton warhead ever be used against a military target without unlawfully affecting protected citizens?

PLOWSHARES VS. DEPLETED URANIUM: Early in the morning on December 19, 1999, the fourth Sunday of Advent, Philip Berrigan and Susan Crane, plowshares activists from Jonah House; Fr. Steve Kelly, SJ. who non-cooperated with probation restrictions upon his release from prison for the Prince of Peace Plowshares action; and Elizabeth Walz, a Catholic Worker from Philadelphia, entered the Warfield Air National Guard Base in Middle River, Maryland. They hammered and poured their blood on two A-10 Warthog (Fairchild Thunderbolt II) aircraft. They sought to disarm the A-10 for these planes are equipped with a Gatling gun which fires 3,900 rounds of depleted uranium (DU) per minute. DU is a dense radioactive waste product and heavy metal that is used in munitions because it can burn its way through tank armor and oxidizes, releasing radioactive particles up to 25 miles away. When ingested, these toxic particles cause chemical and radioactive damage to the bronchial tree, to kidney, liver and bones, causing somatic and genetic trauma. Cancer often results. DU is not only toxic to people but also poisons the environment. The A-10's fired 95% of DU in Iraq leaving behind over

300 tons of this poisonous element. Over 10 tons of DU was used by the U.S. in Yugoslavia.

As Federal Air Police arrested them, Steve was pepper-sprayed and Susan was tackled. They were then jailed, pending trial.

On March 20 their jury trial commenced in Baltimore County Circuit Court. Prior to the trial, Judge James Smith granted the prosecutor's In Limine Motion, which amounted to a "gag order" against the defendants. Consequently, the defendants would not be allowed to explain why they disarmed the A-10's or call expert witnesses.

On March 22, when the defense called Dr. Doug Rokke, a veteran and foremost expert on DU, the judge found his testimony inadmissible in advance. Susan's testimony was severely restricted, and when she refused to answer who drove the group to the base, the judge called a recess. Susan then informed the judge that because of the extreme repressive nature of the trial they would no longer participate in the proceedings. Then, supporters began to speak out against the court's suppression of the truth and chanted, "I drove the van." As some supporters were being removed from the court by marshals, Steve read from the scriptures, followed by singing from supporters. When the trial resumed, the defendants refused to return to court and remained in their holding cells in the courthouse. After closing statements by the prosecutor, the case went to the jury. After 4 1/2 hours the jury could not agree on a bogus assault charge that had been filed against Susan. A mistrial was declared on that charge and the prosecutor stated he would not retry her in the future. The four were all convicted of malicious destruction of property—with property damage of more than $300 and conspiracy to maliciously destroy property. Phil was sentenced to 30 months imprisonment,

THE PLOWSHARES CHRONOLOGY 1980-2003

Steven and Susan to 27 months, and Elizabeth to 18 months. They were also each ordered to pay one-fourth of $88,622.11, and should they be released pending appeal, each would need to post $90,000.

In their action statement the group declared "We come...to convert the A-10, as Roman Catholic Christians, in obedience to God's prohibition against killing. Also, to embody Isaiah's vision of a disarmed world where hearts are converted to compassion and justice and the weapons are converted to tools of peace. Finally, to atone for another nuclear war in Iraq, and a third in Yugoslavia. So help us God."

On January 3 and 12, 2001, Crane and Berrigan were released from prison on third party custody pending a probation revocation in Portland, Maine for the violating the terms of their sentence for the Prince of Peace Plowshares action. On February 2, 2001, appearing before their original sentencing judge, Gene Carter, they answered charges of committing a crime, associating with felons, and not paying restitution. They were each sentenced to one year in prison and immediately incarcerated. They were both released from prison on December 14, 2001. In August, Kelly was released from his Maryland prison sentence and placed immediately into federal custody. Because he could not guarantee he would report voluntarily for his probation violation hearing in Maine, he was jailed until his September 25 hearing. On October 10 he was sentenced to 14 months imprisonment.

SILENCE TRIDENT PLOWSHARES: On June 24, 2000, Michael Sprong, co-publisher of Rose Hill/Fortkamp Books and peace activist, and Bonnie Urfer, member of NukeWatch and peace activist—both from Luck, WI, entered the ELF site near Clam Lake, WI. In an act of disarmament and crime prevention, they used hand-held Swede saws to cut down three poles supporting the transmission lines for the U.S. nuclear submarine communication system, taking the transmitter off-line. They attached references to laws and treaties to the poles they cut. In their action statement they declared that their action was justified because Project ELF is an imminent threat to people and the environment. They waited for over an hour for Ashland County Sheriff Deputies to arrive, who then took them into custody. This is the fifth time since 1984 that the ELF transmitter has been shut down by activists who simply walked up to poles supporting the 28-mile-long transmitter antennae and cut them down with handsaws.

A witness to the action, Barbara Katt, of the Anatoth Community in Luck, was also taken into custody on suspicion of being "party" to the alleged crime.

The following day, ten supporters held a support vigil at the ELF site. Annika Spalde and Kate Berrigan were arrested for delivering an indictment that was carried by Bonnie and Mike on June 24. They were charged with trespass and jailed until the following night.

At the first hearing for Mike, Bonnie and Barb on June 27, Barb was released for lack of probable cause. Mike posted $1000 bond and was released. Bonnie was denied bond and ordered held on outstanding warrants, each from previously unpaid Project ELF protest fines. She was released after a week. Due to information that the U.S. District Attorney's Office would prosecute the case, the Ashland County District Attorney declined to prosecute the two on a state charge of intentional damage to property. On Oct. 18, the two were informed that they will be charged in U.S. District court with "willfully injuring property belonging to the U.S. department of the Navy". This Federal misdemeanor charge carries a maximum penalty of a 1 year prison sentence.

On February 20-21, 2001, Bonnie and Mike were tried by a jury in Federal Court in Madison, Wisconsin. In pre-trial orders presiding Magistrate Crocker ruled "irrelevant and inadmissible" any and all testimony or evidence referring to Project ELF, Trident submarines, nuclear weapons policy, international law, the laws of war, or the U.S. Constitution, which explicitly elevates treaty law above all federal statutes. During the trial, jurors watched a 25 minute videotape of the action made by activist Barb Katt. The video was

THE PLOWSHARES CHRONOLOGY 1980-2003

taken as evidence when Katt was apprehended at the action site, and presented as part of the prosecutor's case. While the video showed Bonnie and Mike posting a Citizens' Indictment citing these documents and the word "Nuremberg" clearly painted on the sawed down pole, neither the indictment nor the Nuremberg Principles were allowed as evidence or seen by the jurors.

The Magistrate did permit the "advice of counsel" defense, which might excuse a crime if the defendants acting in good faith believing the competent legal advice of an attorney that a certain act would be lawful. But Crocker called for a strictly abbreviated version of such testimony. Bonnie and Mike testified about the advice given them by several lawyers, including Anabel Dwyer, an adjunct professor of International Human Rights law who helped argue the International Court of Justice case regarding the use and threat of nuclear weapons. They argued how the actions they took to stop the annihilation of life on earth was lawful and necessary under International law and Article VI of the U.S. Constitution asserting that treaties endorsed by the U.S. are the "supreme law of the land." The jury took three hours before rendering a guilty verdict. On May 4 Bonnie was sentenced to six months in prison and ordered to pay restitution of $7.492.44 and given 1 year supervised release. She was immediately incarcerated. Mike was sentenced to two months imprisonment, the same amount of restitution and one year supervised release.

SACRED EARTH AND SPACE PLOWSHARES: On September 9, 2000, the 20th anniversary of the Plowshares Eight action, five Roman Catholic Sisters from several religious communities entered Petersen Air Force Base in Colorado Springs where some 150,000 visitors were attending "The Spring 2000 Department of Defense and Open House and Air Show." Jackie Hudson, OP, from the Ground Zero Community in Poulsbo, Washington; and previous plowshares participants Carol Gilbert, OP, Ardeth Platte, OP, Anne Montgomery, RSCJ and Liz Walters, IHM, proceeded to hammer and pour their own blood on a Milstar Communications satellite receiver and an F-18 (Hornet) fighter plane used extensively in Iraq. They struck the plane and nearby satellite receiver four times each—for a total of twenty times, to commemorate 20 years of plowshares-disarmament actions. They also unfurled a banner with the inscription "Sacred Earth and Space Plowshares 2000." After hammering on the plane, the Sisters prayed the Lord's Prayer and read their action statement which declared: "We reject the U.S. Space Command Vision for 2020: To dominate space for military operation...to exploit space for U.S. interests and investments...to waste billions and billions of dollars and more human and material resources, causing the destruction of

Sacred Earth & Space
PLOWSHARES 2000

the Earth and desecration of Space...Our security is neither in wealth nor in war. It is the God of the universe who calls us to 'act justly, to love mercy, and to walk humbly with our God'... In this spirit we act as an invitation to all to 'hammer swords into plowshares...that nation will not lift up sword against nation nor will they ever again be trained to make war.' " The Sisters were arrested, jailed and charged with federal criminal mischief, obstructing government operations and two counts of conspiracy. Troubled that there were Sisters in his jail, the commander of El Paso County Jail stated: "I have heard reports from supervisors that the ward has never been quieter. There are special prayer groups going on. But I have a problem with nuns being in my jail." The five Sisters were all unexpectedly released from jail on Sept. 16 and their charges were surprisingly dropped.

JUBILEE PLOUGHSHARES 2000: Early in the morning on November 3rd, 2000, Fr. Martin Newell, a Catholic priest from London, England and Susan van der Hijden, a Catholic Worker from Amsterdam, Holland, entered the Wittering Air Force Base in Cambridgeshire, England. Seeking to enact the biblical prophecy to "beat swords into plowshares," the two proceeded to disable a convoy truck being prepared to carry nuclear warheads for Trident nuclear submarines to Faslane, Scotland, the home-port for four British Tridents. They hammered inside the truck on the dashboard and on other equipment in the back of the vehicle. They also painted the words "The Kingdom of God is among you," "Drop the debt, not the bombs," and "Love is the fulfillment of the law." The two then went in search of security personnel to inform them of their action, whereupon they were arrested and imprisoned. The two were charged with burglary and two counts of criminal damage totaling 32,000 British pounds. At a January 5th court hearing the two pleaded not guilty to these charges.

In their action statement they declared: "We have acted in a spirit of repentance for our complicity in crimes against humanity and God. We have acted to uphold the law. Through the Jubilee 2000 campaign, the church has committed herself to working for justice for the poor and oppressed. British nuclear weapons are a central part of the chains of oppression. As Christians we have taken responsibility and acted in solidarity with the least of the world."

On May 25, they were tried in the Chelmsford Crown Court in Essex, England. During their four day jury trial, they were both able to testify about their intent and how they acted to prevent a crime. Several witnesses were also able to offer limited testimony. The judge refused to allow the defendants and their lawyers legal arguments based on the illegality of Trident under international law. In her closing statement, Susan pointed out that there had been several acquittals of Trident activists in England and implored the jury to do what was right according to their own hearts. In his final instructions the judge told the jury not to consider the defense of necessity or defenses related to protecting property or crime prevention. Though they were found guilty by a majority verdict, two jurors acted on their conscience and refused to convict. Susan and Martin were sentenced to one year imprisonment and were freed because they had already served seven months in prison. They were placed on probation for the remaining five months of their sentence.

HMS VANGUARD DISARMAMENT ACTION: April 26-27, 2001, Ulla Roder, mother and member of the Trident Three Disarmament action, swam undetected for five hours past police launches, over a floating barrier and into the high security berth where Tridents are docked at the Faslane Submarine Base in Scotland. She made her way to where two Tridents were berthed, the HMS Victorious and the HMS Vanguard. Carrying a chisel and hammer she placed the chisel between two tiles on the sub which are used to help it remain undetected from enemy craft. As she lifted her hammer from the water a very nervous soldier, removing the safety catch and pointing his machine gun directly at her, ordered her to "get away from the submarine." When she informed him that she was a peace protester, he still persisted in his order. As another nearby guard sounded a security alarm, she proceeded to comply with the soldier's order and moved a meter back from the sub. When the soldier seemed calmer, she drifted near the Trident and spray painted "USELESS" on the side of the submarine. From the water she shouted that the soldier should not be proud of his job preparing for mass murder. Ministry of Defense police arrived and she was placed under arrest. She was charged with malicious damage, breach of by-laws, and being inside a prohibited area without authorization. She was released from police custody after four hours. She was tried and convicted in mid-September and sentenced on October 5 to three months in prison. She was jailed until October 29, and released under the threat of deportation.

SACRED EARTH AND SPACE PLOWSHARES II: On October 6, 2002, at 7:30 a.m., three Roman Catholic Dominican Sisters and members of the Sacred Earth and Space Plowshares action in 2001, Carol Gilbert, Jackie Hudson and Ardeth Platte, entered Minuteman missile silo site N-8 near Greeley, Colorado. Wearing white mop-up suits which said Disarmament Specialists and Citizens Weapons Inspection Team, they cut through two gates and entered the silo area. They hammered on the tracks used for the silo lids to open and on the silo itself. They also used their blood to make the sign of the cross on the tracks and on the silo. They then began defencing-- cutting through the fence in three places. They concluded the witness with a liturgy. By 8:30 a.m. military personnel arrived in humvees with machine guns pointed at them and they were placed under arrest.

THE PLOWSHARES CHRONOLOGY 1980-2003

They were then taken to the Womens Detention Center in Greeley. They appeared in state court the next day and were charged with destruction of property--this charge was dropped when their case was transferred to federal court. On October 16, 2002, they appeared in Denver Federal Court and were initially charged with destruction of government property. Although she did not participate in the action due to her peace-work in Hebron with the Christian Peacemaker Team, Sr. Anne Montgomery signed the action statement. In their statement they declared: We, women religious, come to Colorado to unmask the false religion and worship of national security so evident at Buckley AFB, in Aurora, the Missile Silos, and in Colorado Springs: Schreiver AFB (the Space Warfare Center), the Air Force Space Command Center at Peterson AFB, Cheyenne Mountain (NORAD) and the Air Force Academy. We reject the mission of these along with the U.S. Space Command and Stratcom in Omaha, Nebraska...We act in the many names of God the Compassionate, ar-Rahim: our Life, our Peace, our Healer to transform swords into plowshares, our violence and greed into care for the whole community of earth and sky, not as masters but as servants and friends.

On October 24, they were arraigned in federal court in Denver and were given two charges: "Injury/Obstruction of National Defense of the U.S." which carries a maximum sentence of 20 years imprisonment and a $250,000 fine, and "Injury to Government Property of the U.S." which carries a 10 year sentence and $250,000 fine. They refused a personal recognizance bond because of restrictions the court imposed prohibiting them from participating in further protests. They remain imprisoned and their trial began on March 31, 2003. During an extremely repressive week-long jury trial, the judge and the prosecutor denied them the opportunity to present their moral and legal justification defenses to the jury. They were convicted of all charges and are awaiting sentencing.

SHANNON PLOUGHSHARES: On January 29, 2003, Mary Kelly from the Shannon Peace Camp, hammered on the nose, nose wheel and the hydraulics of a U.S. Navy C-40 Boing 737 aircraft from the 59th Fleet Logistics Squadron that was based at Shannon Airport in Ireland. Such planes are used to transport troops, weapons and ammunition to the Middle East. She was arrested and charged with causing damage to the plane equal to about 500,000 euro. She was held in prison for several weeks and then released on bail pending trial.

PIT STOP PLOUGHSHARES: In the early morning on February 3, 2003, five peaceworkers affiliated with the Catholic Worker: Deirdre Clancy, Karen Fallon, Damien Moran, Nuin Dunlop and ploughshares activist Ciaron O'Reilly, cut through a fence and made their way to the runway at Shannon Airport. They poured their own blood on the runway that has been servicing U.S. military flights, troops, and munitions deployments to U.S. military bases in Kuwait and Qatar. They constructed a shrine on the runway to Iraqi children killed and threatened by U.S./British bombardment and sanctions. The shrine consisted of copies of the Bible and Quran, rosary and Muslim prayer beads, flowers, photos of Iraqi children and St. Brigid crosses. They also began to take up part of the runway with a mallet.

They then approached a hanger housing a U.S. Navy plane under repair. They pained "Pit Stop of Death" on the hanger's roller door, and began the dismantling of the hangar. Others entered the hanger to disarm the repaired U.S. warplane. They were arrested by police and refused to cooperate with bail conditions. They were remanded to prison where they initiated a fast for peace and called for mass nonviolent resistance to Irish complicity in the forthcoming war against Iraq. As of this writing a trial date has not been set.

In their action statement they declared: "The Irish government acts in contravention of the Irish Constitution, International Law and divine mandate to service U.S. military aircraft, troops and munitions deployments...We come to Shannon Airport around the Feast of St. Brigid, to disarm and disable the war machine. We hope to begin to take up the runway and ground military aircraft...We find this easier to envision than the further slaughter of Iraqi children that U.S., British and Irish governments wish us to consider...We act inspired by Brigid and Irish traditions of healing and peacemaking. We carry out Christ's command to "love our enemies" by nonviolently resisting the slaughter of their children. We attempt to enflesh the prophecy of Isaiah and Micah "to beat swords into ploughshares." Caoimhe Butterly, a peace activist who was shot in the leg by the Israeli military while doing solidarity work in the West Bank, signed her name as a co-conspirator to the action. All but Karen are out of jail.

NATO PLOUGHSHARES: On February 9, 2003, Barbara Smedema, a member of the Dutch Peace Action Camp, entered a NATO airbase in Vokel, Holland. Protesting the looming war against Iraq and the alleged existence of nuclear weapons stored by NATO at the base, she used a sledgehammer to damage three satellite dishes. She was arrested, detained by military police and taken to a jail in Uden. She was charged with endangering flight traffic, being a member of a criminal organization and damaging government property. She is scheduled to appear in court on February 19, 2003.

9-11 AND THE GOSPEL
IMPERATIVE OF NONVIOLENCE

By Arthur Laffin

Although many people, including religious leaders, supported the U.S. war in Afghanistan and the new so-called war on terrorism in response to the 9-11 attacks, the Dorothy Day Catholic Worker, of which I am a member, has joined with numerous people of faith and conscience in calling for no retaliation and no war. These have included family members of victims of 9-11 like Amber and Ryan Amundson and Mr. and Mrs. Rodriguez and other members of Peaceful Tomorrows.

Those who profess to be Christians must first look to Jesus as the moral reference point regarding how we should respond to the 9-11 attacks. If we truly believe that Jesus is the Messiah, the Savior of the world, then we must follow His Gospel. At the heart of the Gospel are the following commands: *"You shall love the Lord your God with all your heart, with all your soul, and with all your mind, and with all your strength,"* and that *"You must love your neighbor as yourself. There is no other commandment more important than these two"* (Mk.12:30-31). Jesus further declares: *"You have heard that it was said 'You shall love your neighbor and hate your enemy.' But I say to you, love your enemies and pray for those who persecute you"* (Mt. 5:43-44).

With respect to the practice of forgiveness Jesus says, *"Be merciful just as your Father is merciful"* (Luke 6:36) and, *"Forgive, and you will be forgiven"* (Lk. 6:37). He calls us to forgive seventy times seven (Mt. 8:22). Jesus also forgives the woman caught in adultery and about to be stoned. He beckons those about to stone her: *"Let anyone among you who is without sin be the first to throw a stone at her"* (Jn. 8:7). Jesus most powerfully demonstrates the meaning of forgiveness when he is crucified. As he is dying on the cross Jesus prays to God for those murdering him, *"Father, forgive them; for they do not know what they are doing"* (Lk. 23:6).

Regarding the use of weapons, during Jesus' arrest when one of the disciples strikes the slave of the high priest, cutting off his ear, Jesus declares: *"Put your sword back into its place, for all who take the sword will perish by the sword"* (Mt. 26: 52). Then Jesus quickly proceeds to heal the slave's ear.

To illustrate the importance of not making hypocritical judgments, Jesus asserts, *"Why do you see the speck in your neighbor's eye, but do not notice the log in your own eye? Or how can you say to your neighbor, 'Friend, let me take out the speck in your eye,' when you yourself do not see the log in your own eye? You hypocrite, first take the log out of your own eye, and then you will see clearly to take the speck out of your neighbor's eye"* (Lk. 6:41-42).

Nowhere in the Gospels does Jesus instruct his disciples to be vengeful or to kill. Rather, Jesus calls his followers--then and now--to practice the same unconditional love that he shows us, especially on the cross. Jesus calls us to follow him and no other earthly power. He calls us to deny ourselves, and take up the cross--which means that we must be willing to be persecuted and even give our lives out of obedience to God.

Jesus does not teach a "just-war" or "just-killing" theory. Jesus teaches a love ethic which includes loving our enemies. Therefore we cannot profess to follow Jesus while at the same time, demonizing, bombing, and killing our neighbor. We cannot be complicit in or silent about killing. Every person is made in God's image. We are all children of the same God regardless of our race or religion. All life is sacred; no person is expendable. An Afghan or Iraqi life is as precious before God as an American life. If we kill one person we kill a part of God. Thus any act of killing, by an individual, group or state blatantly violates God's command *"Thou shalt not kill."*

It is because of my faith in Jesus that I vehemently denounce the horrific violence carried out by the suicide hijackers. This same faith requires that I denounce the U.S. war against Afghanistan and Iraq and oppose all war and killing.

I continue to mourn for the victims and pray for all who have suffered the heartbreaking pain of losing loved ones at the World Trade Center, the Pentagon and in Pennsylvania. I know this pain all too well as my brother, Paul, was murdered in 1999. The pain and grief others and I have felt about the attacks, however, is not a cry for war. It is instead a cry for mercy and a plea for justice that is rooted in compassion. The biblical call of forgiveness and reconciliation has been of immense help to me and numerous others to heal from the wounds of violence.

Tragically, we are now experiencing the same terror on U.S. soil that many people in different places in the world know so well. As we try to understand 9-11 we need to discern the root causes for why people are driven to carry out violent acts against the U.S. We must also recognize that the epidemic of violence we see in our society mirrors the violence the U.S. government uses when it sanctions killing and uses lethal military means to enforce its will around the world. We must understand, too, that the U.S. practices terrorism by its lethal first-use nuclear posture and by its acts of military intervention. Since 1900 the U.S. government has engaged in over 100 acts of military intervention worldwide. The U.S. has also spent $20 trillion on the military budget since the 1940's. And, according to the Pentagon, there are currently U.S. troops stationed in 150 countries. Violence begets violence. The use of violence and weapons can never make us secure or bring about a just peace. Long-time peacemaker Elizabeth McAlister asserts, *"There is no security and there is no defense except the works of justice."* (1)

I believe that the guiding moral principle for responding to the 9-11 attacks must be based on the divine command *"Thou shalt not kill."* This means that we cannot kill or support killing under any circumstance. The bombings carried out in Afghanistan by the U.S. and its allies, which has so far killed over 4,000 people, decimated Afghanistan's infrastructure, and caused severe environmental destruction, betray the Gospel. International Red Cross facilities and emergency food and refugee supplies were destroyed by U.S. bombs. The U.S. also used cluster bombs and "fuel air bombs" or "daisy cutters" which can kill every creature within a square mile radius of the impact point. These 15,000 pound bombs explode and spread a fine kerosene vapor into the atmosphere. A secondary explosion then ignites the fuel vapor, creating a massive pressure wave. Anyone caught in the conflagration is incinerated and the blast wave sucks out oxygen behind it, creating a vacuum that ruptures lungs. These and all other such weapons are immoral. It is insidious for President Bush (who was selected not elected) to have asked American children to donate $1.00 to help Afghan children when the U.S. was bombing their country and displacing them.

What do we do about those who commit violent crimes? I believe the Gospel calls for holding people and governments accountable for their actions and practicing "restorative," not retributive justice. We must condemn the sin but not the sinner. We must never use violence or killing as a means to redress an act of injustice or violence. No matter how long it takes, we must use nonviolent and diplomatic measures to respond to the suicide attacks and all other conflicts. Military tribunals, racial profiling, torture and the illegal jailings of numerous Arabs and Muslims living in and outside the U.S. are irreconcilable with the Gospel tenets of restorative justice.

We must also honestly look at how millions of people have been killed worldwide by acts of military violence and economic systems of exploitation, including actions carried out by the U.S. government. I have personally witnessed the devastating effects of U.S. policies in Central America and the Middle East. In 1998, I went to Iraq with a Voices In The Wilderness delegation--in violation of U.S. sanctions law. During my visit I met Iraqi children dying from severe malnutrition, preventable diseases and the cancerous effects caused by U.S. depleted uranium weapons. They are among the more than one million Iraqis, mostly children, whom UNICEF estimates have died as a direct result of twelve years of U.S.-led U.N. economic sanctions and from the effects of U.S. and British bombings. These sanctions, which are the real weapon of mass destruction in Iraq, and ongoing bombings are war crimes and must end immediately.

We can't have one standard of "justice" to address one crime and another standard to address another crime. We must be careful not to be hypocritical and practice a double standard. We must first take the log out of our own eye before we see clearly to take the speck out of our neighbor's eye.

If the cycle of violence is to end in our world, the U.S. must do its part and take responsibility for the violence it has caused. I believe the U.S. government, which Martin Luther King, Jr. described as the *"greatest purveyor of violence in the world,"* should repent and ask forgiveness for how it has caused the suffering and death of people in our own land and around the world. This would include Native Americans and African Americans, as well as peoples from Hiroshima and Nagasaki, Vietnam and Southeast Asia, Central and South America, Africa, Panama, Vieques, Iraq, the former Yugoslavia and Afghanistan.

Furthermore, an international Truth and Reconciliation Commission, like that created in South Africa, should be established to address violent crimes carried out by governments, corporations, groups and certain individuals. The goals of such a commission would be, in part, to publicly hold accountable those who have committed atrocities, to provide assurances that a just restitution be made to the victims and ultimately, to attain reconciliation between the perpetrators of the crime and the victims and their families. This commission could be comprised of past Nobel Peace laureates, women and men from each continent involved in human rights and conflict resolution work, religious leaders and international law experts.

Finally, the U.S., which comprises six percent of the world's population yet consumes nearly half of the world's resources, must cease exploiting poorer nations. The U.S. must also stop supporting corrupt regimes, selling arms, training foreign soldiers to terrorize and kill their own people at the now renamed School of the Americas and elsewhere, and using its military might to enforce and protect its interests, especially oil in the Middle East and Central Asia. It is extremely hypocritical for the U.S., the preeminent nuclear superpower and arms dealer in the world, and the only country to have ever used nuclear weapons, to tell another country, like Iraq, to disarm when it refuses to abolish its own nuclear arsenal and biological and chemical weapons. As the world's richest nation and leading superpower, the U.S. must disarm, demilitarize, abolish all weapons, call for the just redistribution of the world's resources, protect the environment, end racism, and develop a foreign policy that respects the human rights of all people. And it must cease its quest for empire. Pursuing these and other steps would help foster a new climate of hope and stem the terror and fear now engulfing our world.

Taking such measures would certainly have a positive effect toward resolving the conflict between Israel and Palestine. If there is to be an end to the violence and a just peace between Israel and Palestine, the U.S. must stop sending weapons and military aid to Israel, call for Israel to end its illegal occupation of Gaza and the West Bank, call for the immediate implementation of U.N. resolution 242 and other U.N. resolutions, and genuinely support self-determination for the Palestinian people.

Instead of pursuing a path of peace and calling for the abolition of war, President Bush stated on December 26, 2001 that 2002 would be a "war year." Thus the Bush Administration has promulgated an "axis of evil" ideology and has declared to the nations of the world that "*you are either with us or against us*" in the war against terrorism. To wage this war, Bush and the Congress will spend over $379 billion on the military budget in 2003 and some $400 billion in 2004. In the same way past presidents used the specter of "communism" to justify massive military increases and covert and overt interventionary wars, Bush is now using the threat of "terrorism" to justify exorbitant military spending, Star Wars and the Ballistic Missile Defense program, new weapons, interventionary wars in Columbia, Iraq and elsewhere, launching pre-emptive strikes and using nuclear weapons against its adversaries, as well as suspending certain civil liberties. Thus, using terms like "terrorism" and "axis of evil" only perpetuates a climate of fear, mistrust and division and serves as a guise for U.S. aspirations of global domination.

As I write, the Bush Administration, despite massive worldwide opposition, has initiated a new war against Iraq. The primary reason for a U.S. invasion and regime change in Iraq is the same reason the U.S. has waged war against Iraq for the last twelve years: OIL. Control of Persian Gulf oil has been, and continues to be, the driving force behind U.S. policy in the Middle East. Prior to the Gulf War (massacre) in 1991, President George H.W. Bush stated: *"Our way of life...will suffer if control of the world's great oil reserves fell in the hands of...Saddam Hussein."* (2) Also General Norman Schwarzkopf, chief U.S. military commander of the Gulf War, asserted in 1990: *"Mideast oil is the West's lifeblood. It fuels us today, and being 77 percent of the free world's proven oil reserves, is going to fuel us when the rest of the world has run dry...It is estimated that within 20-40 years the U.S. will have virtually depleted its economically available oil reserves, while the Persian Gulf region will still have at least 100 years of proven oil reserves."* (3) And on September 15, 2002, the Washington Post ran a front page story titled "In Iraqi War Scenario, Oil Is the Key Issue." This article detailed how U.S. oil companies stand to profit from a U.S. take-over of Iraq. Thus, the U.S. invasion of Iraq has resulted in the slaughter and displacement of numerous Iraqis and the destruction of Iraq's society. It is a colossal sin and war crime.

We are at a critical turning point in history. Will we continue the cycle of violence and injustice which will only lead to a spiral of resentment and violence, and even to the possible use of biological, chemical and nuclear weapons? Or will we choose a nonviolent path that growing numbers of people worldwide now advocate? Martin Luther King warned that the choice before us is no longer between violence and nonviolence; it is a choice between "nonviolence or non-existence."

Nobel Peace Laureate Mairead Corrigan Maguire declares: *"If we want to reap the harvest of peace and justice in the future, we will have to sow seeds of nonviolence today. It is the only hope for the world."* I am convinced that the way of nonviolence, most radically exemplified by Jesus, is the only way out of our culture of violence and the present crisis we face. I believe personal and societal transformation is possible if we place our complete trust in God, follow God's commands and boldly act on what we say we believe. Radical changes have occurred throughout history. Slavery and apartheid have been abolished and the Berlin Wall has come down. And all over the world today courageous actions abound for nonviolence, disarmament, economic justice, human rights and safe-guarding the environment.

The challenges before us are great but not insurmountable. Let us never forget that God is with us and that through God's amazing grace, miracles can occur. Now more than ever we must avail ourselves to God's grace and create a life-affirming alternative to the dehumanizing and violent world we live in. In all we do we must espouse the way of nonviolence, community, social justice, servant-hood, sharing, cooperation, simple living, a reverence for all creation, forgiveness and reconciliation. We must also refuse to participate in, pay for or support in any way the systems of domination which exploit, kill, pollute and wage war.

Daniel Berrigan, internationally renowned priest, peacemaker and poet, reminds us that *"our plight is very primitive from a Christian point of view. We are back where we started. Thou shalt not kill; we are not allowed to kill. Everything today comes down to that—everything."* (4) Thus, now more than ever, out of obedience to God and on behalf of the victims, we must resist all violence, killing and war-making, and beat all swords into plowshares. The reign of God is at hand! God is sovereign over all earthly powers. God, not presidents, judges, corporate heads and generals, will have the last word! Believing that with God all things are possible, mindful that the cloud of witnesses is at our side interceding for us, let us pray for faith and courage to be God's peace and justice-makers.

<u>NOTES</u>

1. McAlister, Elizabeth, National Catholic Reporter, 9/21/01, p. 8
2. Blum, William, Killing Hope, (Monroe, ME: Common Courage Press), 1995, p. 329
3. Ibid. p. 330
4. Berrigan, Daniel, The Catholic Worker, December, 2001, p. 6

RESOURCES

BOOKS

Ackerman, Peter and Jack Duvall, *A Force More Powerful: A Century Of Non-Violent Conflict* (New York: St. Martin's Press), 2000

Berrigan, Philip and McAlister, Elizabeth, *The Time's Discipline: The Beatitudes and Nuclear Resistance* (Baltimore: Fortkamp Publishing Co.), 1989

Berrigan, Philip, *Fighting the Lamb's War* (Monroe, ME: Common Courage Press), 1996

Berrigan, Daniel, *To Dwell in Peace* (San Francisco: Harper and Row) 1987

Bertell, Rosalie, *Planet Earth: The Latest Weapon of War* (London: The Women's Press), 2000

Boyle, Francis, *The Criminality of Nuclear Deterrence* (Atlanta: Clarity Press, Inc.), 2002

Boyle, Francis, *Defending Civil Resistance Under International Law* (Dobbs Ferry, NY: Transnational Publishers Inc.), 1987

Blum, William, *Killing Hope: U.S. Military and CIA Interventions Since World War II* (Monroe, ME: Common Courage Press), 1995

Chomsky, Noam, *9/11* (New York: Seven Story's Press), 2001

Clark, Ramsey, *The Fire This Time: U.S. War Crimes in the Gulf* (New York: Thunder's Mouth Press), 1992

Consedine, Jim, *Restorative Justice* (Lyttleton, New Zealand: Plowshares Publications), 1999

Day, Sam, *Crossing the Line* (Baltimore: Fortkamp Publishing Co.), 1991

Dear, John, *Peace Behind Bars* (Kansas City: Sheed and Ward), 1995

Dear, John, ed., *Henri Nouwen: The Road to Peace* (Maryknoll, NY: Orbis Books), 1988

Dellinger, Dave, *From Yale to Jail* (New York: Pantheon Books), 1993

Douglass, James, *The Nonviolent Coming of God* (Maryknoll, NY: Orbis Books), 1991

Ellsberg, Robert, *All Saints* (New York: Crossroads), 1998

Ellsberg, Robert, ed., *By Little and By Little: Selected Writings of Dorothy Day* (Maryknoll, NY: Orbis Books), 1992

Gandhi, Mohandas K., *Nonviolent Resistance* (New York: Shocken Books), 1967

Grossman, Karl, *The Wrong Stuff: The Space Program's Nuclear Threat to Our Planet* (Monroe, ME: Common Courage Press), 1997

Hallock, Daniel, *Hell, Healing and Resistance: Veterans Speak,* (Farmington, PA: Plough Publishing House), 1998

Herngren, Per, *The Path of Resistance* (Philadelphia, PA: New Society Publishers), 1993

Howard, Donna and Tom Hastings, *Laurentian Shield: Nonviolent Disarmament of Nuclear Navy in Wisconsin* (Available at STOP Project ELF, 740 Round Lake Rd., Luck, WI, 54853)

King, Martin Luther, *Strength to Love* (Philadelphia, PA: Fortress Press), 1982

Laffin, Arthur and Anne Montgomery, *Swords Into Plowshares* (S. Dakota: Rose Hill/Fortkamp), 1996

McCarthy, Colman, *I'd Rather Teach Peace* (Maryknoll, NY: Orbis Books), 2002

McSorley, Richard, *New Testament Basis of Peacemaking,* (Scottsdale, PA: Herald Press), 1985

McSorley, Richard, *It's a Sin to Build a Nuclear Weapon* (Baltimore: Fortkamp Publishing Co.), 1991

Merton, Thomas, *The Nonviolent Alternative* (New York: Farrar, Straus and Giroux), 1980

Myers, Ched, *Who Will Roll Away the Stone?* (Maryknoll, NY: Orbis), 1994

Naar-Obed, Michele, *Maternal Convictions: A Mother Beats a Missile Into a Plowshare* (Maple, WI: Laurentian Shield Resources for Nonviolence), 1998

Nelson-Pallmeyer, *School of Assassins* (Maryknoll NY: Orbis Books), 1997

Norman, Liane Ellison, *Hammer of Justice: Molly Rush and the Plowshares Eight* (Pittsburgh: Pittsburgh Peace Institute), 1989

O'Grady, Jim and Murray Polner, *Disarmed and Dangerous: The Radical Lives and Times of Daniel and Philip Berrigan* (New York: Basic Books), 1997

O'Reilly, Ciaron, *Bomber Grounded: Runway Closed* (South Dakota: Rosehill Books), 1994

Wilcox, Fred, editor *Disciples and Dissidents: Prison Writings of the Prince of Peace Plowshares* (Athol, MA: Haley), 2000

Wylie-Kellermann, Bill, ed., *A Keeper Of The Word: Selected Writings Of William Stringfellow* (Grand Rapids, MI: William Eerdmans), 1994

Zelter, Angie, *Trident on Trial*, (Edinburgh, Scotland: Luath Press Limited), 2001

Zinn, Howard, *A People's History of the United States* (N.Y.: Harper Colophon), 1980

OTHER RESOURCES

The Catholic Worker Bookstore, P.O. Box 3087, Washington, DC 20010 [202-722-1911]
A project of the Peter Maurin Center, the Catholic Worker Bookstore carries and sells a wide range of books by noted authors on peace, justice and nonviolent resistance.

The Nuclear Resister, P.O. Box 43383, Tucson, AZ 85733 [520-323-8697] Publishes a regular tabloid chronicling anti-nuclear and anti-war nonviolent resistance actions in the U.S. and abroad and maintains current addresses of imprisoned resisters.

PLOWSHARES SUPPORT GROUPS

Jonah House, 1301 Moreland Ave., Baltimore, MD 21216 (Publishes regular newsletter, *Year One*, offers support to plowshares prisoners).

Kairos New York, 618 W. 138th St., Apt. #4, New York, NY 10031 (Maintains resources on the plowshares actions, including audio-visual resources, supports plowshares prisoners).

Dorothy Day Catholic Worker, 503 Rock Creek Church Rd. NW, Washington, DC 20010 (Publishes *The Little Way* and supports prisoners).

Trident Ploughshares 2000. A British-based nonviolent direct action campaign to stop the Trident submarine. Publisher newsletter, *Speed the Plough*. Maintains web site: www.gn.apc.org/tp2000. 42-46 Bethel St., Norfolk, NR2 INR. England.

WEB SITES

The Plowshares Chronology Online
www.plowsharesactions.org

Trident Ploughshares 2000
www.gn.apc.org/tp2000/

Swedish Plowshares
www.plowshares.se/english/index.htm

The Nuclear Resister
www.nonviolence.org/nukeresister

The Catholic Worker Bookstore
www.catholicworker.com/bookstore

London Catholic Worker
http://www.geocities.com/londoncatholicworker

PHOTO INDEX

*Arthur Laffin is a member of the Dorothy Day
Catholic Worker in Washington, DC*

THE PLOWSHARES CHRONOLOGY 1980-2003
[99]